# TOWARD
# THE
# COMMON
# GOOD

*Everyone is called to serve
the community. . . .*

## REV. JOHN FORLITI

**BROWN-ROA**
*A Division of Harcourt Brace & Company*

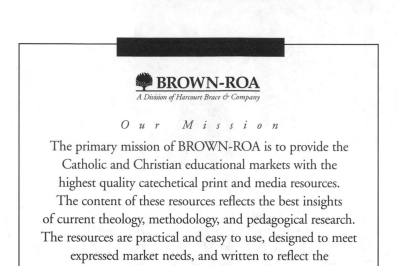

**BROWN-ROA**
*A Division of Harcourt Brace & Company*

*O u r    M i s s i o n*

The primary mission of BROWN-ROA is to provide the
Catholic and Christian educational markets with the
highest quality catechetical print and media resources.
The content of these resources reflects the best insights
of current theology, methodology, and pedagogical research.
The resources are practical and easy to use, designed to meet
expressed market needs, and written to reflect the
teachings of the Catholic Church.

Requests for permission to make copies of any part of the work should be mailed to:
Permissions Department, Harcourt Brace & Company, 6277 Sea Harbor Drive,
Orlando, Florida 32887–6777.

Excerpts from *Economic Justice for All* Copyright © 1986 United States Catholic
Conference, Inc., Washington, DC. Used with permission. All rights reserved.

Printed in the United States of America

ISBN  0-15-950589-5

3 4 5 6 7   129   08 07

# Preface

These reflections originally appeared in the weekly bulletin of Saint Olaf Catholic Church in downtown Minneapolis. They are offered again in this book as a resource to individuals and groups wanting to promote the building up of our social fabric. After all, neighborhoods, communities, and cities are the "homes" where we live. If "caring" is the ingredient which transforms a house into a "home," then why is it not also true for our neighborhoods, communities, and cities?

The common good is the overarching theme of these reflections. Simply stated, the common good is the "greater good"; it happens when individuals place their own personal good second to the good of the community. There is a gnawing conviction in my heart which believes that we have become too tolerant of behaviors which poison society. The problems seem overwhelming, too massive for any one person to do anything about, and trying to work together often comes to a standstill.

Diversity, individual and personal rights, cultural differences, various value and belief systems all seem to get stuck at the point of individual agendas. We need a new starting place. Could it be the common good?

The themes offered here will stimulate some conversation. The discussion questions will encourage more. Neither is presumed to be the last word. That, the last word, is in your hands. Hopefully, it will be the decision to act, to commit to the common good and to work for its up-building.

John E. Forliti
April 12, 1998

# Contents

# Foreword

Catholic social teaching is a central and essential element of our faith. Its roots are in the Hebrew prophets who announce God's special love for the poor and call God's people to a covenant of love and justice. Our social teaching is solidly rooted in the life and words of Jesus Christ, who came "to bring glad tidings to the poor—liberty to captives—recovery of sight to the blind."

Our Catholic social teaching is a call to compassion and respect for all people. Issues of race, national origin, economic status, and the things that potentially divide us can be the very issues which can unite us if our hearts are rooted in the gospel. Our teaching proclaims that we are brothers and sisters and that we are a part of the human family created by God. Essential to all of this is the common good. We are not only sacred, but we are social, and human life is life in community. The obligation to love our neighbor certainly is an individual dimension. It also requires a broader social commitment, and that's what we really mean by the common good.

Father John Forliti's book is a much-needed and masterful presentation of this whole concept. Further, his own pastoral skills and instincts make this book not only readable, but wonderfully applicable to daily life.

Archbishop John R. Roach

# Questions *for Reflection following a* Christian Service Action

1. **Motivation for service**
   - For what reason did I begin this action?
   - What feeling or emotion accompanied my beginning?

2. **The experience itself**
   - What sights, sounds, smells, tastes, touches remain with me from the experience?
   - What incident is a highlight for me as I recall the experience?
   - What feelings or emotions did I experience during the action?
   - What would I do differently next time? What would I change?

3. **Ongoing impact**
   - Is this a one-time event or something I choose to incorporate into my future?
   - How will I connect this event with my personal prayer and integrate it into my spiritual life?
   - What life choices will I make differently in the future in light of this experience?

# Reclaim
# *Our Community*

A month ago I happened upon a friend from the East Coast. When I mentioned that I was from Minneapolis, he quickly responded, "You mean Murderapolis!" I was not amused. Obviously he was referring to the published fact that currently our murder rate is higher than New York City's!

Then this morning's news headline revealed the startling fact that drug use and abuse among the nation's teenagers has risen dramatically. Not good news. One immediate and predictable comment on the radio was that the answer lies in more alcohol and drug education in our schools. I winced. We've tried education, and it's not enough.

Don't get me wrong. Prevention programs are important and indeed necessary; however, they are not the critical key. Education presumes good will as well as the capacity to be virtuous. Some individuals have neither. They are a danger to society and need to be appropriately restrained.

Granted, the murder rate and teen drug use both reflect complex problems. But the factor which is too often ignored or bypassed in considering either of them is the factor of sanctions: society's negative consequences for offenders. Some individuals simply do not get the message without paying some kind of price first. I submit that, without rules and sanctions, education is not enough to meet the needs of all children and youth. The same goes for a good number of adults, as well. Some people simply do not get the message unless they feel some pain: loss of privileges, a fine, incarceration, shame, discomfort, something that catches and holds their attention.

What can we do to help our community regain its good reputation? I believe we need to keep our institutions strong: our government, police, schools, and religious institutions. We need to hold everyone accountable for making our community a safe place for everyone. The gangs that have established a foothold must be uprooted and thrown out. If the police and the courts need more effective tools to make this happen, let's give them what they need. If the teachers and principals in our schools need more authority and support to root out gangs and drugs, let's be sure they have it. If delinquent parents need more support in the disciplining of their children, holding them more accountable will help, but they'll need support.

As our nation searches for safer and more healthy neighborhoods, let's not forget the lessons of common sense. Bad apples do spoil the barrel. Rules are essential to community. So is effective enforcement. Let's give the authorities in our midst the support they need to do their jobs. On the one hand, we expect people in authority to protect us; on the other, we tie their hands!

*But seek the welfare of the city where I have sent you into exile,*
*and pray to the LORD on its behalf,*
*for in its welfare you will find your welfare.*
**Jeremiah 29:7**

# From the Catholic Tradition

. . . *the teachings of the Church insist that* government has a moral function: protecting human rights and securing basic justice for all members of the commonwealth [Peace on Earth, *60–62*]. *Society as a whole and in all its diversity is responsible for building up the common good. But it is government's role to guarantee the minimum conditions that make this rich social activity possible, namely, human rights and justice [Vatican II, "Declaration on Religious Freedom"* (Dignitatis Humanae), *6. See John Courtney Murray,* The Problem of Religious Freedom, *Woodstock Papers, no. 7* (Westminster, MD: Newman Press, 1965)].

**U.S. Bishops, *Economic Justice for All* (1986), 122.**

# For discussion

1. Twenty-three centuries ago, a Greek philosopher taught that knowledge and virtue are two different things. We know this is true in our own lives. What are examples from your life experience in which knowing something is right doesn't automatically translate to someone's doing it? What can "tip the balance" and assist a person to put into action what one **knows** to be true?

2. In addition to education, such as drug or sex education courses, several other factors can significantly influence human behavior. Some of these may be sanctions or punishments, role models or mentors, moral convictions, religious beliefs, and peer pressure. To what extent does our present education system incorporate these factors? How do you build these other important factors into an educational program? To what extent do these factors affect your own life?

3. What supports do people in authority—in education, law enforcement, human services, or in families—need to more effectively fulfill their roles? In what ways do structures prevent them from functioning at their best? What kinds of supports would assist them most? What is the role of a morally healthy person who is subject to authority?

4. Does your religious community include prayer for the city in its worship service? Do you include this in your personal prayer? Why or why not?

5. While politicians declare their "get tough on crime" policy, Pope Paul VI declared: "if you want peace, work for justice." How might economic justice promote peaceful neighborhoods?

6. Why do Church leaders insist that capital punishment oversteps the boundaries of appropriate sanctions? What basic justice is at stake?

## To promote the common good, I will

- cast an informed vote in local school board elections or volunteer to campaign for candidates who will promote strong schools.
- pray for the welfare of our city.

## Personal reflection

# Killer
# *Kids*

I did my student teaching at Boys' Totem Town, a residential home for kids caught by the law. It was there that I met for the first time a boy without a conscience. He was twelve years old. He had been picked up for arson, having set ablaze a science museum to the tune of thousands of dollars. He gave no clue that he realized what he had done was wrong. It wasn't that he wasn't bright, he simply had no sense of right and wrong. I wondered then who might be his next victim, because surely there would be others. He was a killer-kid in adolescence. He'd likely stay a killer-kid no matter how old.

People without a conscience—what a frightening reality this is! In 1959, this was a rarity. Not so today! All too regularly the news has stories about senseless rapes, murders, drive-by shootings, and violent acts "just to see what it feels like." This morning's *Pioneer Press* has a gripping editorial cartoon. It's titled "Street Values": heroin, $70–$80/gram; handguns, $50–$100 each; crack, $3–$20 a vial; human life, zero!

I came across this cartoon only moments after I had read the depressing story about the 17-year-old lad who, just days ago in Duluth, barely bumped his car into the back of another car. The five men in that car brutally beat, shot, then dumped his limp body into his trunk, and drove car and victim into a lake. Innocence defiled! Society must find better means of protecting innocent life from people without consciences. Count on it: such deformed humans pose grave potential danger. Without internal restraints, only external restraints will hold them back!

Why does a person grow up without a sense of right and wrong? Bad parenting is one reason: inconsistent and confusing discipline, morally ugly role models, no accountability for one's actions, sanctions which are either inconsistent or lacking altogether. Another reason is that our society has grown more and more permissive, with relativistic values. Killer-kids are left to roam in a no-fault, guilt-free environment. A third reason is our abortion and assisted-suicide mentality. Life doesn't have the absolute respect it deserves.

However they have been spawned, killer-kids need to be in restraints. God may be their judge as to the level of their guilt, but society and its leaders must be their judge as to the level of their freedom. People without consciences can't be educated into civility. Society will be blessed if even incarceration will catch their attention. For sure, sermons by priests or judges or concerned relatives will not make a dent in steeled hearts. As for the present, there is scant hope for their healing. Society can only restrain.

What else society can do is prevent the next generation from producing more killer-kids. There is no substitute for moral training, for wise and prudent discipline which truly teaches an honest sense of right and wrong. Absolute standards are essential, consistency in training is crucial, a belief in God or some supreme order *outside* of oneself is necessary. There is no true morality if there is no external standard to which a person feels accountable.

Those charged with the responsibility to hold kids accountable need the support of the society at large. Let them do their job, and if they don't, replace them with others who will. Kids with killer potential rule by intimidation. A society without the courage to protect itself from them will sooner or later collapse.

*For the Lord honors a father above his children,*
*and he confirms a mother's right over her children.*
**Sirach 3:2**

# From the Catholic Tradition

*We must distinguish between the error (which must always be rejected) and the person in error, who never loses his dignity as a person even though he flounders amid false or inadequate religious ideas. God alone is the judge and the searcher of hearts; he forbids us to pass judgment on the inner guilt of others. The teaching of Christ even demands that we forgive injury, and the precept of love, which is the commandment of the New Law, includes all our enemies.*
**Vatican II, *Church in the Modern World* (1965), 28.**

# For discussion

1. Conscience is traditionally defined as "the voice within" telling a person what is right and wrong. How do *you* define conscience? Compare and contrast a well developed and poorly developed conscience. Identify a historical or fictional character who represents to you a well-informed or badly informed conscience.

2. Identify an example of a consistent standard or a behavioral norm which shapes your community's moral fabric. How healthy or how weak are these standards in your school, your neighborhood, your city?

3. Bad parenting, permissiveness and low respect for human life are three factors which may weaken a community's moral fabric. Rank these factors according to your estimation of their impact on our society's moral climate. Explain why you rank them as you do. Choose one of these factors and discuss how you feel its effects. What other factors weaken our society's moral environment?

4. "You have the right to believe whatever you want." Is this true? What absolute standards are essential for a healthy society? List and discuss personal beliefs which are out of line in a healthy society.

5. The quote from *Church in the Modern World* reminds us to "love the sinner while hating the sin." How does one effectively separate one's regard of an enemy from the wrong the person does?

# I will ensure the common good

- by volunteering as a Big Brother or Big Sister or by assisting a leader of a local scout or other youth group.
- by acting today with personal integrity, refusing to pass judgment on the inner guilt of others.

# Personal reflection

# Excuses
## *vs. Explanations*

Sometimes the simplest distinctions can make a world of difference! All too often, in pastoral work as well as my years as disciplinarian at the high school and college levels, I have met with this all-too-human self-deception: if the doer of wrong can explain his action, he thinks he ought to be excused.

A young man is caught damaging a neighbor's car after a weekend party. "I was drunk," he explains, expecting to be let off the hook. "So . . ." I would respond, "that may explain your irresponsible act, but it doesn't excuse it one bit. Pay the damages, apologize to the car owner, and next time, think twice before you take that first beer!" Case closed.

Explanations may help us understand a behavior, but rarely should they excuse. Times have changed, and not always for the better. These days explanations are too often accepted by too many persons in authority as excuses, and irresponsibility is thus rewarded by the cancellation of a deserved sanction or punishment. Who wouldn't like to weasel out of the negative consequences of bad behavior? The next time you hear someone brag about not being held accountable, would you at least wonder about the impact on the common good?

Our society is struggling to recover from the threat of men and women who would prefer to run from accountability and not "face the music." After all, the moral fiber of a society depends on the moral strength of its individual members. Owning up to the consequences of one's actions is moral strength. Yes, there probably are situations when an explanation might also serve as an excuse, however, this ought to be the exception, not the rule. (This is another curious twist of our culture—making the exception into the rule.)

What do you think? Should producers of violent programs be left off the hook for their destructive impact on our social fabric because, as they like to explain, people want their stuff? Should companies who sponsor such rot be excused for the same or any other reason? Should manufacturers of shoes and clothing be left off the hook as they make millions of dollars off the slave labor of children in Third World countries for whatever economic or other explanation they can muster? Are athletes who lend their mystique to their advertising excused because they give some of their profit to charity? Talk about robbing Peter to pay Paul!

The explanation-serving-as-excuse is a sign of the sickness of our time, and it is hemorrhaging our society. "I'm not rich, so I stole; I got divorced and she got custody—that's why I don't pay child support; he bumped my car so we "capped" (shot) him; no one caught me so it ain't wrong."

Explanations are not excuses. For the common good we simply have to hold others and ourselves accountable to high moral standards.

*Wisdom cries out in the street;*

*in the squares she raises her voice.*

*At the busiest corner she cries out;*

*at the entrance of the city gates she speaks.*

**Proverbs 1:20–21**

# From the Catholic Tradition

*A well-ordered human society requires that [people] recognize and observe their mutual rights and duties. It also demands that each contribute generously to the establishment of a civic order in which rights and duties are progressively more sincerely and effectively acknowledged and fulfilled. It is not enough, for example, to acknowledge and respect every [person's] right to the means of subsistence. One must also strive to insure that [they] actually have enough in the way of food and nourishment.*

**Pope John XXIII, *Peace on Earth* (1963), 31–32.**

# For discussion

1. "There's no excuse for that!" When is an explanation not an excuse? Can an explanation be an excuse? Is there always a reason, even if it is not an excuse?

2. Who calls you to accountability? What is your typical response to correction? What makes you defensive?

3. Whom must you correct or hold accountable? How comfortable are you with this? How do you approach a confrontation of this kind? At what point do you consider that another person's decision is none of your business?

4. As a society, what is our explanation for permitting slave labor of children in the manufacture of our clothing? Is it a legitimate excuse? What is your explanation for purchasing these garments? How do you feel about it?

5. *Peace on Earth* says that we must strive to insure that all people actually have enough in the way of food and nourishment. Still 40,000 die daily due to malnutrition. What efforts can and do we make toward the welfare of the starving? What more could we do? What explanations/excuses are given around this topic?

# I will encourage respect for the common good

- by participating in Bread for the World's Offering of Letters. (For information contact Bread for the World, 1100 Wayne Avenue, Suite 1000, Silver Spring, MD 20910; phone 301-608-2400; www.bread.org.) Bread for the World is a Christian citizens' movement seeking justice for the hungry.

- by learning about sweatshop conditions overseas by viewing a video such as *Zoned for Slavery*, produced by the National Labor Committee (NLC). (For information contact NLC, 275 7th Ave., New York, NY 10001, phone 212-242-3002, www.nlcnet.org.) The NLC is a human rights advocacy group promoting and defending worker rights.

# Personal reflection

# Respect

The judge asked the juvenile why he shot and killed a guy. "He dissed me," came the reply. "Dissed" is a slang word meaning disrespected. So that's what our community has come to—a young tough takes offense and thinks he has the right to take a life.

The philosopher Dietrich von Hildebrand taught that reverence (respect) is the mother of all virtue. Let us make no mistake about it. Respect seems to be in very short supply in our society: respect for those in authority, respect for elders and the aged, respect for life, respect for one's self, respect for our essential institutions, respect for God, respect for police, respect for the environment—the list is long.

Perhaps what many are confusing is this: All of God's creation has a right to be respected simply by its being. God didn't make junk, the '60s poster declared. Right on! But we humans are capable of making junk, and a lot of it is our bad behavior, which doesn't deserve respect.

No question about it, every human being is deserving of respect and has a right to it. That's elemental, basic, at the core of human dignity, and God-given. But not every human act is worthy of respect. Respect for behavior has to be earned! Drug use, exploitation of another, the irresponsibility of dead-beat dads, white-collar crime, acts of injustice, use of foul and uncivil language—such behaviors do not deserve respect. It's the old adage come into play: Love the sinner, but despise the sin.

Easier said than done, I suspect, because separating one's actions from one's being requires some sophistication. For example, a person who is habitually dishonest or unjust, we correctly describe as a dishonest or unjust person. To a great degree, actions do define our identity. That's why it's so difficult to maintain respect for people whose behaviors are despicable. Yet we must keep trying to love the person while hating the behavior.

On the side of the bad actor, he or she finds it similarly difficult to maintain self-respect when she or he is told consistently, "You are bad," although it's actually the behaviors that are bad. Good behaviors make for self-esteem and a healthy self-respect, while bad behaviors plunge one's self-respect downward. It's true that honest actions do build into an honest person, and *vice versa*.

What's all this got to do with the common good? The more common the virtue of respect exists for both person and morally good behavior in our society, the better off everyone will be. We must begin with the respect that flows from human dignity— every human person has a right to a fundamental respect simply from her or his being a person. However, behaviors are quite another thing, which is why it's so important to understand that respect based on behavior is something that has to be earned.

The killer-kid who took a life because someone hurt his feelings could not have had a clue as to what respect truly is.

*Confuse, O Lord, confound their speech;*
*for I see violence and strife in the city.*
*Day and night they go around it on its walls,*
*and iniquity and trouble are within it.*
**Psalm 55:9–10**

# From the Catholic Tradition

*. . . the common good requires the social well-being and development of the group itself. Development is the epitome of all social duties. Certainly, it is the proper function of authority to arbitrate, in the name of the common good, between various particular interests; but it should make accessible to each what is needed to lead a truly human life: food, clothing, health, work, education and culture, suitable information, the right to establish a family, and so on . . . the common good requires peace, that is, the stability and security of a just order. It presupposes that authority should ensure by morally acceptable means the security of society and its members. It is the basis of the right to legitimate personal and collective defense.*
**Catechism of the Catholic Church, #s 1908–1909.**

# For discussion

1. Respecting another person not only does *not require* your respecting his or her bad behavior, it requires your *not respecting* the bad behavior. Explore this. Cite examples of bad behavior which appeared in the news this week. What is your response to these news items?

2. Why is it difficult to respect a person whose behavior is despicable? Explore the relationship between *being* and *doing*, human dignity and human behavior. For example, how can this affect a family group which includes a "black sheep" or non-conforming member?

3. Respect based on behavior has to be earned. Not so with respect for being human. Why is this distinction crucially important? Is this distinction sometimes blurred, and with what results? List several attacks on human dignity evident in our contemporary world. Which three are most serious? Explain your thinking.

4. What bad behaviors are most troublesome to you in your circle of friends or co-workers? How do you deal with these behaviors? How are these behaviors disturbing the peace which must undergird the common good?

5. Can a person be robbed of human dignity? Why or why not?

6. Reflect on these words of Aleksandr Solzhenitsyn: "If only there were evil people somewhere insidiously committing evil deeds, and it were necessary only to separate them from the rest of us . . . but the line dividing good and evil cuts through the heart of every human being. And who is willing to destroy a piece of their own heart?" How do you compare or contrast his thought to the reality of "killer kids?" Does evil reside within our hearts? Explain your answer.

# I will facilitate the common good

- by apologizing to someone to whom I showed disrespect.
- by volunteering to assist in a group home, sheltered workshop, or on a retreat for mentally challenged individuals. (For further information, contact your diocesan office.)

# Personal reflection

# Beyond
# *Tough Love*

Recently I spent an evening visiting a homeless shelter and the Salvation Army's Harbor Light facility on the edge of downtown Minneapolis. The shelter is operated by Catholic Charities; it's an emergency service directly resulting from the closing of the former Drake Hotel shelter. This new "safe" shelter, together with Harbor Light, hosts a community of some five hundred adults, not all of them inside! The lawn along the Harbor Lights building is where those who can't get into either facility end up for the night, sleeping outside on a patch of lawn, with nothing to protect them from the elements of nature or society. It isn't a pretty sight, and it's a disgrace for the richest nation in the world.

The people who staff these facilities and others like them throughout our metro area are some of the real heroes among us. Their burn-out rate is telling. Most of their clientele are the poorest of the poor, the Gospel poor who will always be with us. Some suffer from mental disorders or diseases, others from the effects of addictions, others from abusive relationships, some simply had a streak of bad luck.

Whatever the case, most, if not all, of these folks feel desperately disenfranchised from society and are immobilized, at least for now, by a deep feeling of hopelessness. Many are hanging on to life by a thin thread of structure leavened with compassion which the social workers and shelter staffs provide. These servants of the city who do "front-line" duty assisting the poor deserve our prayers and support.

I spoke with one staff person who had been still caught up in the homeless lifestyle himself only two years ago because of chemical addiction. He credits the court system with saving him. Its demands and requirements pushed him into treatment for the third time, and it finally worked. He will be grateful for the rest of his life. Staffing the shelter reminds him daily of the people who did not quit caring about him. "If it's the fiftieth time an addict is put into treatment, we can't give up," he says, "because we don't know which time the treatment will take."

At a time in our history when we know that tough love has its place in helping people grow healthy and well, we must never quit being compassionate. Life in the shelters and on the street is not an answer to anything. It certainly does not contribute to human dignity. Neither is it an example of how a civilized society (especially one so incredibly blessed and rich) should treat its "orphans and widows" and disenfranchised brothers and sisters.

My visit to the homeless community on Currie Avenue was but a brief glimpse of human suffering. Yes, I believe the welfare system needs reform. Which system doesn't? As our society does the reforming, however, let us not lose our compassion, especially for God's poor who absolutely need another person's helping hand. For some, society's help will always be required. Others, thankfully, will move out of homelessness and hopelessness.

Let's keep our compassion level high, making certain that tough love doesn't become an excuse for hardness of heart. A society that has no room for its broken members is spiritually bankrupt and is the poorer for it. That's not an outcome the welfare reforms should have. We must do better than providing a patch of lawn at the edge of downtown.

*Do not add to the troubles of the desperate,*
*or delay giving to the needy.*

**Sirach 4:3**

# From the Catholic Tradition

*Christians believe that Jesus' commandment to love one's neighbor should extend beyond individual relationships to infuse and transform all human relationships from the family to the entire human community. Jesus came to "bring good news to the poor, to proclaim liberty to captives, new sight to the blind and to set the downtrodden free" (Luke 4:18). He called us to feed the hungry, clothe the naked, care for the sick and afflicted, and to comfort the victims of injustice (Matthew 25). His example and words require individual acts of charity and concern from each of us. Yet they also require understanding and action upon the broader dimensions of poverty, hunger, and injustice which necessarily involve the institutions and structures of economy, society, and politics.*

**U.S. Bishops, *Political Responsibility* (February 1976), 6.**

# For discussion

1. There will always be some people in a community who cannot care for themselves. They call for and have a right to the compassion of others. Why is "tough love" not appropriate in these cases? Recall words and actions of Jesus which shed light on the Christian response to these poor.

2. Who do you imagine to be a worthy recipient of welfare? Who is unworthy?

3. What stereotypes do you, your friends, your co-workers, have about those who are poor or homeless, or persons on welfare? What is a stereotype and what effects do they have on the common good?

4. Describe a comfortable, ideal home. Should everyone have a home? Is a home different from housing? Explain your answer.

5. Would it be possible for everyone in the world to live in a "dream" home? Why or why not? Does my purchase of little luxuries affect those who are homeless? Why or why not? How does my being a Christian shape my spending choices? Should being a Christian make a difference in personal purchases?

# I will stimulate a commitment to the common good by

- by assisting or visiting a local homeless shelter or "soup kitchen" project.
- by learning about and donating money to the work of Catholic missionaries to bring compassion and justice to the world's poor (e.g., Maryknoll Office of Global Concerns, PO Box 29132, Washington, DC 20017; www.maryknoll.org).

# Personal reflection

# Authority

I learned in college that the first duty of authority is to establish itself. A few years later, when I began to teach high school sophomores, I began to believe it. Authority hates a vacuum. This simply means that if the teacher doesn't run the class, the students will! A teacher who does not establish clearly, within the first week of school, that he or she is the authority in the classroom is in for a very long year.

The principle works for authority of all types. Parents who take their parental authority lightly discover that their kids do likewise. CEOs, managers, and other authority figures in the business world who prefer to be buddies rather than bosses learn quickly that authority not established is authority ignored. The buck does have to stop somewhere.

Since the 1960s authority has taken more than its share of lumps. Watergate didn't help, nor did the upsurge of sex-abusers (coaches, teachers, clergy, and so on), nor did people in high places with immoral egg on their faces. It wasn't necessary for society to overreact, but it did: by knocking down every authority pedestal it could find. Suddenly, it seemed, parents didn't know how to parent anymore, teachers teach, or presidents preside. As for the police, well, they were submerged in subliminal, if not overt, negative stereotypes. Soon the traditional respect authority once had fell victim to minimalization. Society woke up one day to discover that the runts had taken over the rule.

Among the most noxious of the runts are the gangs. To their credit they are making it abundantly clear in Minneapolis, St. Paul, and suburbs that our once safe cities have a serious authority problem. For the common good, we had better restore ample respect for the police. This includes giving them greater benefit of the doubt when they exercise judgment, as any authority must, in carrying out their duties. When second-guessed constantly by no lesser authorities (e.g., judges, journalists and the media), it might just be that the wrong people are being handcuffed!

Another area where the runts are ruling has been in some of our neighborhoods. Guns and knives in schools are hardly subtle signs that principals and teachers better be given back their authority to run the schools, which includes disciplining effectively.

Happily there are signs that our society is catching up to the authority vacuum, one being the Mall of America's recent decision to encase the place with a curfew. Good move. Sure, some good kids are being punished, too, by the new curfew rules, but for the common good, this had to be. That's precisely what the common good can sometimes require, namely, that individuals give up something in order that the larger group be served.

For the common good, authority is absolutely essential. For authority to work for the common good, it must first establish itself, meaning that those in authority must accept their authority, make it understood, and make it stick. Back in the '60s when the pendulum swung, it swung too far, as pendulums always do. Bringing it back to the center may take a bit more time. It will certainly take more courage.

*When the righteous are in authority,*
  *the people rejoice;*
*but when the wicked rule,*
  *the people groan.*

**Proverbs 29:2**

# From the Catholic Tradition

*Society cannot survive without authority, which derives from God and promotes the common good (46). Thus authority must have moral power to oblige, a power coming from God and used in accord with right reason (47). Civil authority's chief means of moving men must be, not punishment or reward, but appeal to individual consciences; human dignity rules out any man's coercing another to perform interior acts (48).*

*Human authority's power to oblige in conscience comes only when it is related to God's (49). Human dignity is thus protected, since men reverence God by their obedience to others—and, in so doing, ennoble themselves (50). Since authority derives from God and the moral order, no law or command can oblige when it contradicts that order or God's will (51). Though authority comes from God, it does not therefore follow that men lack freedom to choose their rulers or government in a truly democratic way (52).*

**Pope John XXIII, *Peace on Earth* (1963).**

# For discussion

1. According to *Peace on Earth*, what is the source of real authority? What is the difference between genuine authority and mere power? What happens to society when those in authority fail to establish their authority? How does this affect the common good? Choose a person in authority whom you respect and identify the characteristics of this person which earn your respect.

2. For the common good, it is unfortunate but necessary sometimes that the innocent suffer a loss of privileges (e.g., the curfew at the mall). Feeling his or her "rights" to be violated in such instances, an "innocent" person might sue. From the perspective of the common good, why would such a lawsuit be ill-advised? How do you feel about youth curfews? Why? Are unannounced locker searches in high schools a violation of personal rights or a legitimate use of authority?

3. Do gangs function with authority, with power, or with both? Why do you answer as you do? In your opinion, why do gangs attract new members?

4. What gave Jesus authority? Explain your answer giving specific examples from the Gospels.

5. *Peace on Earth* (51) allows for legitimate civil disobedience. What is civil disobedience? Speaking historically, when has it been used? Why, for instance, did Rosa Parks refuse to move to the back of a segregated bus?

# I will study choices made for the common good

- by informing myself about the social problem of gangs and working with my community to provide wholesome outlets for youth.

- by researching public policy statements on crime (c.f. www.policy.com).

- by investigating draft resistance. (For more information from a faith perspective: Fellowship of Reconciliation, P. O. Box 271, Nyack, NY 10960; 914-358-4601; www.nonviolence.org//for/.)

# Personal reflection

# Basic *Morality*

Have you ever tried to gather good people together and construct a statement of commonly held values, upon which you *all* agreed, and succeeded? I have tried, and it's always much more work than it should be, it seems. We sit there, each of us, wanting to articulate the deepest values within our hearts, but wanting also not to have to give up anything in the process.

If the basic moral law is indeed "written on our hearts," then why can't basically good humans agree on what's written there? Agree, for instance, on statements such as:

- Do unto others as you would have them do unto you.
- It's wrong to steal, cheat, be dishonest, be unjust.
- It's right to keep promises made, to be faithful to one's spouse and family, to be a good neighbor to one in need.

Human history reveals a constant struggle within communities large and small over the contents of what is written in our hearts. This struggle itself is perhaps the greatest proof we have that there is, indeed, a natural moral law fixed in the nature of things by the One who created us.

And that's the simple truth: the Creator is the One who made the moral dimension we find so essential, yet so perplexing. Our Creator placed within the human race the capacity to choose between good and evil, the power to do right and to do wrong. Because the moral law is written in our hearts, as individuals we can and do look to our consciences for guidance on moral issues. But we also look to the conscience of the larger community. Both "looks," individual and social, work correctly, for the most part, but there are failures in both. Acquaintance rape and apartheid serve as stark reminders of each, respectively.

Social conscience, like individual conscience, is a creation of God. We need it to guide the more social aspects of our lives. Communities collapse without it. Any society unable or unwilling to articulate the basic God-given moral law and hold its common set of moral principles will surely know more chaos than it needs to.

The way through much of our struggling with social morality is to look to our religious traditions. Even here the journey is not without fault; religious wars are one obvious example of failure within our religious tradition. Still, our religious traditions are the best we have. They are the most obvious means God has given us to find the best moral path. The closer we come to God's word written on our individual *and collective* hearts, the better off we'll be. Our nation was founded upon the Judeo-Christian revelation and its collective wisdom. As other world religions blend their wisdom into our nation's social fabric, I am confident that we will find the One God to be the source of what's written in their hearts as well. Multi-culturalism and diversity need not be a barrier to society's articulation of our commonly held values.

For people of faith, no matter what faith tradition it is, our religious traditions must be our starting point. We need never back away from its guidance, even when challenged on the basis of separation of church and state. The wall of separation was put there to protect our religious traditions, not to bury them. Social morality, like individual morality, must begin with the Creator of all, who gave us humans our moral capacity. Let's not hesitate to articulate our commonly held moral values. For God's sake and the sake of all peoples, let's not fail to pass them along to the next generation!

*I will put my law within them,*
*and I will write it on their hearts;*
*and I will be their God,*
*and they shall be my people.*

**Jeremiah 31:33**

# From the Catholic Tradition

*Permit me to enumerate some of the most important human rights that are universally recognized: the right to life, liberty and security of person; the right to food, clothing, housing, sufficient health care, rest and leisure; the right to freedom of expression, education and culture; the right to freedom of thought, conscience and religion; and the right to manifest one's religion either individually or in community, in public or in private; the right to choose a state of life, to found a family and to enjoy all conditions necessary for family life; the right to property and work, to adequate working conditions and a just wage; the right of assembly and association; the right to freedom of movement, to internal and external migration; the right to nationality and residence; the right to political participation and the right to participate in the free choice of the political system of the people to which one belongs.*

**Pope John Paul II, *Address at the United Nations* (1979), 13.**

# For discussion

1. Beside the suggested examples of the moral law listed in the second paragraph on page 25, what other examples of the moral code are written on our hearts?

2. According to the Catholic bishops, working for justice is a "constitutive dimension" of our faith. What does this mean? How can an individual person work to promote justice or human rights? How can a religious community do so?

3. Research the "Golden Rule" (Do unto others as you would have them do unto you) as it is found in other faith traditions. What does it suggest about the One God? What value or danger is there in learning about other religious traditions?

4. Do you agree that religious wars represent a failure of a religious tradition? Why or why not? Choose a religious war, past or present, to illustrate your stand.

5. What is "consensus decision making"? What are its advantages and disadvantages? How does it relate to the word of God as found in a group's collective heart?

# I will initiate action for the common good

- by writing a letter to appeal for human rights in a situation of injustice. (Contact Amnesty International for information on "Urgent Actions": Amnesty International USA, 304 Pennsylvania Ave. SE, Washington, DC 20003; www.amnesty.org.)

- by expressing appreciation to a person whom I consider an unsung community hero.

- by participating in a decision-making process which is governed by principles of consensus rather than Robert's Rules of Order.

# Personal reflection

# Institutions

Imagine your body without bones. Could you walk anywhere, reach for anything, do aerobics? Imagine your body without skin? What would hold it together? Imagine your body without blood vessels, veins and arteries doing their job of keeping you alive and nourished. Without a blood system functioning reasonably well, we wouldn't survive.

I think crazy thoughts like this every now and then, not to torture myself, but simply to be reminded how important the institutions in our society are. The systems which keep our body social and our body politic healthy and well are exact parallels to what keeps our physical bodies functioning.

Without our families, without our Churches, without our government, we could not function even reasonably well as a society. Humans are naturally religious and social creatures. These primary institutions come naturally to us.

Tell me that institutions are not essential? They are. Without them we collapse; we can't function as a society; we are dead as community.

Then why doesn't everybody care about our institutions? For one reason, our times are still stuck on the individual, the I-me-mine preoccupation! But, thank God, lots of people do care, or we'd be in tougher shape as a city, state, and nation. So, a thousand thanks to those who work to build up our essential systems and to those who, if they must criticize, do so out of greatness of heart, not smallness.

We need our institutions, and we need them to be strong. Family is the most basic institution. There is little question that much of our current societal collapse can be traced to family breakdown. So bless the husbands and wives and kids who hang in there to keep their marriages and families together. Easy divorce is not healthy for society. Bless our religious institutions. They have kept ideals and moral values and human compassion at the heart of who we are as a people. Benign neglect of religion is not healthy for society. And yes, bless the citizens who are willing to risk losing privacy and peace out of a desire to serve as government leaders. Someone has to do it. Apathy is not healthy for a society. We need as good a government as we can achieve.

What I worry about is how many of us take our institutions for granted. We expect them to work for us at the same time as we conveniently forget that they are us! I feel it often as a religious leader. I see good folks enjoying the benefits which organized religion brings to their lives but acting as if support for our religious institutions comes out of thin air! Rarely do good things happen automatically. Good people make them happen.

Citizens who do not promote family, who do not encourage good government, who do not involve themselves in their church, are missing the everyday opportunities God gives them to build a better world. Our institutions are as strong as we make them.

*The Lord created human beings out of earth,*
*and makes them return to it again.*
*He gave them a fixed number of days,*
*but granted them authority over everything on the earth.*
**Sirach 17:1–2**

# From the Catholic Tradition

*Profound and rapid changes make it particularly urgent that no one, ignoring the trend of events or drugged by laziness, content himself/herself with a merely individualistic morality. It grows increasingly true that the obligations of justice and love are fulfilled only if each person, contributing to the common good, according to his/her own abilities and the needs of others, also promotes and assists the public and private institutions dedicated to bettering the conditions of human life.*
**Vatican II, *Church in the Modern World* (1965), 30.**

# For discussion

1. Primary social institutions are family, religion, and government. How are these more basic even than education and business? The Vatican II document states that each of us is obliged by justice and love to contribute to the common good of families, religion, and government. How do you or could you at your present age or personal development contribute to each institution?

2. Commitment to individuals, though essential, goes only so far. Also essential is commitment to institutions. Reflect on a teacher's commitment to education as well as to his or her individual students; a parent's commitment to family as well as to each child, to marriage as well as to one's spouse. Explore the relationship between commitment to an individual and to a pertinent institution. When does a person have a right or an adequate reason to break his or her commitment to the institution (e.g., to seek a divorce)?

3. Individuals are part of certain basic institutions, but often take them for granted. What are the institutions in which you participate? Assess your appreciation of the institutions in your life. Do you take them for granted?

4. What pressures or forces contribute to a breakdown of the family in our society? What can be done to correct this?

# I will assist in the development of the common good

- by involving myself in my parish, my youth group, my campus ministry.

- by treating my family this week in some special way.

- by supporting the work of Friends Committee on National Legislation to promote Christian values in government. (Information: FCNL, 245 Second Street NE, Washington, DC 20002-5795; 202-547-6000; www.fcnl.org/pub/fcnl/index.html.)

## Personal reflection

# Community
# *Development*

The results from a recent survey of Minneapolis business owners revealed a high number considering a move to the suburbs. That would be unfortunate. Our core city needs local businesses to help anchor neighborhoods. I have believed this for some time but never so deeply as after I met John Perkins and read his book, *Beyond Charity.*

Perkins is an African American born in Mississippi in the 1930s. We met recently at Urban Ventures in south Minneapolis. What a powerhouse! As a deeply committed Christian and as an expert in community development, he has given more than thirty years of his life to the re-building of communities in Mississippi and California, communities gutted by poverty, gangs, economic depression, and the flight of the middle class.

Perkins and Urban Ventures are both worth knowing about. Directed by Rev. Art Erickson, Urban Ventures is in the process of revitalizing ten square blocks on Fourth Avenue south of Lake Street in Minneapolis. Its goal is to recreate a sustainable community, free of drugs and crime. It seeks to establish residents who own their houses, create industries which provide living-wage jobs, and support community stakeholders who work for the common good. It's a noble gamble, and it's taking shape gradually, driven by the vision, hard work, and strong Christian faith of many participants.

Perkin's belief is that inner cities threatened toward collapse do not have to succumb to the inevitable. What has worked for him in the places where he has given his visionary leadership are the three "R's": relocation, reconciliation, and redistribution. Relocation is the movement of committed Christians into an inner city area, Christians whose lives are "together," and who have the personal strength, moral commitment, and strong faith to sustain the gospel into reality. He believes that religiously motivated individuals are the *only* hope for effective community development to take place.

The second "R" is reconciliation. The barriers of race, religion, and social status must be broken through. The gospel of Jesus Christ can serve as a powerful force for good in bridging gaps of all kinds and gathering diverse peoples around a common faith. This happened in the civil rights movement under Martin Luther King Jr. A shared faith was the engine that powered the movement, kept it nonviolent, and provided the vision of a promised land. Perkins has made it happen in his communities.

The third "R" is redistribution. Perkins describes it this way. "Christ calls us to share with those in need. This means redistribution of more than our goods; it means a sharing of our skills, technology, and educational resources in a way that empowers people to break out of the cycle of poverty." Ownership is the key: ownership of homes, of the means of production, and of goods and services. In a capitalistic society, that's simply how it works.

Urban Ventures brings John Perkins to Minneapolis now and again to seek his advice and to be inspired by his life and message. He does have some answers for the building up of the common good. The challenges are many and often over-whelming, but nothing that people of faith can't handle. Urban Ventures is living testimony to what Christ is doing in and through his disciples, all for the common good of a neighborhood, with powerful effects spilled over to the larger community.

> The LORD is the strength of his people;
>   he is the saving refuge of his anointed.
> O save your people, and bless your heritage;
>   be their shepherd, and carry them forever.

**Psalm 28:8–9**

# From the Catholic Tradition

*Economic principles flowing from Catholic teaching:*

1. *Economic activity should be governed by justice and be carried out within the limits of morality.*
2. *The right to have a share of earthly goods sufficient for oneself and one's family belongs to everyone.*
3. *Economic prosperity is to be assessed not so much from the sum total of goods and wealth possessed as from the distribution of goods according to norms of justice.*
4. *Opportunities to work must be provided for those who are able and willing to work.*
5. *Economic development must not be left to the sole judgment of a few persons or groups possessing excessive economic power, or to the political community alone.*
6. *A just and equitable system of taxation requires assessment according to ability to pay.*
7. *Government must play a role in the economic activity of its citizens. Indeed, it should promote in a suitable manner the production of a sufficient supply of material goods. Moreover, it should safeguard the rights of all citizens, and help them find opportunities for employment.*

**U.S. Catholic Bishops, *The Economy: Human Dimensions* (1975), 5.**

# For discussion

1. Explore the meaning and interrelationship of the three "R's" (relocation, reconciliation, and redistribution). How do you think a religiously motivated individual views "redistribution" as opposed to someone motivated in other ways?

2. Why might Perkins be convinced that religiously motivated individuals are the only hope for effective community development? Are there any neighborhoods in your city which need revitalizing? Is there any religious presence there?

3. Name some efforts similar to Urban Ventures in your city or community. What kinds of support do they need?

4. How is work related to human dignity? How does unemployment undermine a sense of human dignity? Explain.

5. What federal economic grants does your city pursue in order to promote basic human rights in its local neighborhoods? What basic human needs are not being adequately met in your community?

# I will communicate the priority of the common good

- by volunteering with or donating to Habitat for Humanity (www.habitat.org) to promote decent housing.

- by attending activities of the local chapter of the NAACP (National Association for the Advancement of Colored People) (www.naacp.org) or other social justice group working toward minority empowerment.

- by learning more about the work of Mother Teresa's order, the Missionaries of Charity, in the United States.

# Personal reflection

# Prevention and *Treatment*

When I was a child, the world around me was heavily into prevention. I remember the tough-talking sermons which railed, for instance, against divorce and against pregnancy outside of marriage. These attitudes extended even beyond the boundaries of religion. The surrounding society generally agreed that breaking up marriages and having children outside of wedlock were not acceptable behaviors. To back up these behavioral ideals, there was significant stigma attached to those not measuring up. This combination of a proclaimed standard and an anticipated shame, along with heavy doses of societal pressure, was a fairly effective means of prevention.

Then things changed—dramatically! In the 1960s, society quickly moved away from a prevention model and moved seriously into a treatment approach. Previously, when divorce or illegitimate pregnancies happened, they were dealt with as matter of fact: "It's unfortunate, but let's make the best of the situation." Now, tough prevention-type talk was seen as downright mean rather than as encouragement toward an ideal. By focusing on the hurt, which was not bad, we lost our conviction about prevention. After all, prevention-talk and the promotion of virtuous ideals in light of human failure can sound harsh, or worse, judgmental. It's not easy to promote an ideal and, at the same time, not cause discomfort to those who have failed.

Before the revolution of the 1960s, when parents would joke to their kids, "Don't do as I do, do as I say," they believed that ideals were terribly important to promote. What's more, they were right, no matter how frequent the failure. Ideals are essential for a society's well-being. Unfortunately, too many people bought the untruth that if you failed to live up to an ideal yourself, you had no business teaching it to your kids. Nonsense!

Our society remains paralyzed over ideals. We have too often given up our responsibility to proclaim them for two not-very-sound reasons: (1) we don't live them perfectly ourselves (as if any human ever could live an ideal perfectly), and (2) we are afraid that by proclaiming an ideal, we may be hurting the feelings of someone who failed to live it.

So we are entangled in a downward spiral. Ideals encourage us to aim high. But we prefer to aim at the average. The sad fact is that if all we do is aim at the average, we will hit lower. Having been in this mode for the past thirty years, we shouldn't be surprised that our standards are plunging. It used to be that norms referred to ideal standards. Nowadays they designate "average," and the average keeps going down.

For the common good, we must recover our ability to state, proclaim, and promote ideals, to aim above average, because plummeting norms are not worthy of human dignity. Without question, treatment is essential when our lives are hurting and life has become a bit unglued. But so is prevention essential, precisely so that fewer lives will become unglued! We must be able to do both. Yes, we have become more sensitive and gotten better at treatment. Can we also recover our skill at teaching ideals, our capacity for prevention?

> *Better is a dry morsel with quiet*
> *than a house full of feasting with strife.*
> **Proverbs 17:1**

# From the Catholic Tradition

*The Church considers it to be undoubtedly important to build up structures which are more human, more just, more respectful of the rights of the person and less oppressive and less enslaving, but she is conscious that the best structures and the most idealized systems soon become inhuman if the inhuman inclinations of the human heart are not made wholesome, if those who live in these structures or who rule them do not undergo a conversion of heart and of outlook.*

**Pope Paul VI, *Evangelization in the Modern World* (1975), 36.**

# For discussion

1. How do you manage the tension between ideals and everyday life, prevention and treatment? Do you think an individual can be happy without ideals to live by? Do you think a society can flourish without shared ideals?

2. What is positive peer pressure? What is negative peer pressure? What connection does peer pressure have to society's standards? Does peer pressure in your local setting encourage teens toward ideals or toward average norms?

3. The Scripture quotation from Proverbs links abundance with strife and tough financial times with peace. Do you think there is a connection between consumption or materialism and society's norms? For instance, do standards slip when money flows freely?

4. Single teen mothers today often choose to keep a child born out of wedlock. Prior to the 1970s they more commonly gave the baby for adoption. In your opinion which choice better promotes the common good?

5. Distinguish the individual's good (whether real or perceived) and the community's good (common good) in the following situations: assisted suicide, gun control, legalized gambling, taxes, environmental legislation, lawsuits, corporate takeovers.

# To promote the common good, I will

- support the services of Birthright to assist unwed pregnant women.

- articulate how individuals benefit when the common good is served.

- learn how Marriage Encounter and Engaged Encounter strengthen the institution of marriage; do this by dialoging with a person who has served on a team.

# Personal reflection

# Homewood

Recently I visited a North Minneapolis neighborhood, took a quick driving tour around its fifty or so city blocks, then had dinner at a local parishioner's home with several guests. The guests were old-timers in that neighborhood, having lived there since the Plymouth Avenue riots of 1968 caught their attention. It was a racially mixed neighborhood already at that time when clusters of homeowners began to meet, determined to make their neighborhood a positive environment for their children and themselves.

I had an eye-opening time at dinner that evening. The story of Homewood, one of the neat neighborhoods of Minneapolis, is cause for celebration. The grassroots folks who pulled together a vision of what they wanted their neighborhood to be for themselves and each other gave the time, energy, and good will to make it happen. As I listened I think I caught several key ingredients which explains their success.

First came the vision. They agreed on what kind of neighborhood they wanted. "Without a vision, the people die," the Bible says! Then came the rest: mutual respect which empowered them to celebrate their differences, the racial mix has hovered about half black and half white; mutual caring which enabled them to simply be neighborly to each other; a communal responsibility for raising their children ("it takes the whole village" concept); a commitment to defend and protect from the threats of illegitimate hell-raisers; a willingness to confront inappropriate behavior; and the courage to demand from the city the services they had a right to receive.

They could have closed their shutters and stayed home and not gotten involved, but they chose rather to work for the common good of the neighborhood. It wasn't easy. Saving their neighborhood from those who would exploit it, damage it, drag it down, required hours and hours of meetings, plus heavy doses of energy and commitment, not in endless chatter, but in projects which were good for the community. Risk-taking became a regular activity, whether it meant speaking out in favor of good ideas or against bad ones, or going out of their way to visit old neighbors and welcome new ones.

In twenty years racism has never been a problem. It might have been! They chose to rise above it. Other differences, too, were celebrated rather than negated: differences in religion, social standing, or economic status. These folks decided to treat each other as neighbors, and they kept their ideals intact. Lots of times it was little things, such as getting to know the names of the neighborhood's children, and making the small talk of conversation which keeps relationships friendly and establishes a basis for mutual trust.

Anyone moving into the area was visited immediately and informed about the community's vision and what behaviors would or would not be tolerated. If a drug house or disruptive situation appeared to be developing, they hounded the police until they got action. Hounding the housing inspector's office also became routine, resulting in the corrective measures required.

It was heartening to see that neighborhoods can be preserved from deterioration. If this is possible for a neighborhood, why not the entire city? The intervention has to be early, however, and the "good guys" have to be strong!

*Whoever winks the eye causes trouble,*
  *but the one who rebukes boldly makes peace.*

**Proverbs 10:10**

# From the Catholic Tradition

*Christian love of neighbor and justice cannot be separated. For love implies an absolute demand for justice, namely a recognition of the dignity and rights of one's neighbor. Justice attains its inner fullness only in love. Because every person is truly a visible image of the invisible God and a brother [or sister] in Christ, the Christian finds in everyone God himself and God's absolute demand for justice and love.*

**Synod of Bishops, *Justice in the World* (1971), 34.**

# For discussion

1. Discuss the key ingredients behind Homewood's success. Which are top priorities? Are there other ingredients not listed?

2. What risks are involved when residents actively work to "save" their neighborhoods? How can those risks be safeguarded? How can children, teens, the elderly assist the process of reclaiming a neighborhood?

3. In Homewood high expectations, coupled with determined action to meet those expectations, led to success. Can you think of other examples where this combination of expectations and follow-through yielded success?

4. Proverbs says that approving a fault causes trouble but honestly confronting it promotes peace. Does a frank reproof cause strife or cure strife? Think of an example which supports your answer. When someone wrongs you, do you usually tend to get revenge, to honestly confront, or to walk away, avoiding conflict?

5. Review your circle of friends. How diverse are they? Describe a friend who is quite different from you, whether that difference is due to age, to race or ethnicity, to background, or to economic level. Why do you love or respect that person?

# I will urge the inclusion of common good in my neighborhood

- by introducing myself to someone I don't know there.
- by participating in meetings of our neighborhood association or organizing an outdoor party for our neighborhood.

# Personal reflection

# Patrol

Last night I went on patrol on the North side. There were twelve in our group, seven pounding the snow-covered pavement, four cruising the neighborhood in a van, and one staffing the walkie-talkie at the "base." This was a "neighborhood patrol night" when volunteer residents walk and ride their streets looking for trouble to nip in the bud.

Probably because the temperature neared zero, the evening was calm. Not many people were out and about. Even so, it was a great learning experience for me. I saw grassroots folks taking responsibility for their neighborhoods, thankful for the support of city-wide projects such as the Neighborhood Revitalization Program, and grateful to a local business for providing space for their police substation.

This substation has been in operation only a year. It's more than a gathering place for nightly patrols. It's also a police presence, and for us, last night, our warming house following the walk. Hot chocolate and cider hit the spot! As I left for home, I took several samples of free literature dealing with a myriad of crime-fighting issues. Educating the local residents is an important objective for neighborhood block clubs.

The evening's experience left me with these impressions. If a neighborhood is to survive the threat of blight, its residents must get to know each other. Char Perry, organizer for her neighborhood, described how big the little things are. One block has a common snowblower they use up and down their sidewalks; many residents have installed outside alarms and neighbors are alert and respond to them. They watch for and report to city inspectors any real or potential violations of codes, and they'll picket absentee landowners' homes if necessary. Working hand in hand with the police and their city council person, the juvenile justice judge has resolved many issues. Taking the initiative is the key to their success so far. There's a war on, and there really are "good guys and bad guys." Who will win?

I'm working from limited knowledge, obviously, so my conclusions may be off. But from what I can gather, at the heart of neighborhood deterioration here are outsiders from other Midwestern cities who have neither the intention nor the capacity to blend in our city as positive and contributing residents. They lack the basic moral values which neighbors must share if any measure of genuine community is to be achieved. The leaders of our city must stir up the will to adequately deal with the criminal element: good police work is only part of the answer. Neighborhood patrols shouldn't be necessary. Judges, probation officers, social workers, politicians, and lawmakers will solve more issues as they collaborate for the common good. If the genie is out of the bottle, those in authority are the ones who must recapture it.

This reversal is not easy if abuse of the welfare system provides sustenance to criminals, if police morale is felt to be gutted by softness at the bench, if the media play to hollow leadership, if neighbors refuse to rise above racism, and if city hall is slow to respond. Over and over I kept hearing from the committed neighbors: accountability. People must be held accountable: residents to be good neighbors, those in authority to do their jobs, and everyone working together for the good of all.

*Unless the* LORD *builds the house,*
   *those who build it labor in vain.*
*Unless the* LORD *guards the city,*
   *the guard keeps watch in vain.*
                                              **Psalm 127:1**

# From the Catholic Tradition

*The rights of the person require that individuals have an effective role in shaping their own destinies. They have a right to participate in the political process freely and responsibly. They have a right to free access to information, freedom of speech and press, as well as freedom of dissent. They have a right to be educated and to determine the education of their children. Individuals and groups must be secure from arrest, torture and imprisonment for political or ideological reasons, and all in society, including migrant workers, must be guaranteed juridical protection of their personal, social, cultural and political rights.*

**Pope Paul VI, *Message Issued in Union with the Synod of Bishops* (1974).**

# For discussion

1. If the system for safety has broken down in your neighborhood, campus, or local school system, who needs to get together to fix it? Identify the "breaks," and the people or persons in authority who can fix it. What can you do to help?

2. Discuss how "reclaiming our community" can include crime prevention efforts at the grassroots level. For instance, how do organizations such as Mothers Against Drunk Driving or Students Against Drunk Driving promote the common good? How many other examples of this type of effort can you name?

3. Morale means a lot. How can you and your community sustain high morale; how can you lift it when it's low: e.g., morale among police, politicians, clergy, social workers, business owners, and so on. How do you raise your own morale when you're feeling down? How do you try to cheer a friend or a relative who is feeling blue?

4. Accountability is critical to healthy community. How is it working in your neighborhood or school or business? How much commitment do you have personally to increasing the overall safety within your neighborhood, campus, or city? What measures can be taken to do that?

5. Something as simple as sharing equipment can strengthen a neighborhood. What else is shared or exchanged in a healthy neighborhood? What stops this sharing from occurring?

6. The pope's statement supports rights for migrant workers. What is your experience of the immigrant workers in your community? Do legal immigrants deserve assistance with food, housing, and medical needs? Do undocumented immigrants have human rights to adequate food, housing, and medical assistance?

# I will activate interest in the common good

- by raising reasonable questions about adequacy of activities and services for young and old.
- by offering to provide a "break" to single moms and adults with dependents.
- by assisting a local battered women's shelter or rape crisis center.

# Personal reflection

# Crime
# *Stopping*

It was a fascinating talk delivered by one of the nation's most creative police chiefs. Ben Greenberg is his name, and he's chief in Charleston, South Carolina. He came to Minneapolis recently to relate some of his success stories. A rising crime rate reversed in his city. Listen to this.

First, their public housing used to be crime-ridden; now it's one of the safest places in the city. Why? The chief says because those in authority decided to be responsible landlords! They began to screen tenants using a list of eleven categories of crime. Applicants with records in any of these categories simply are not accepted into public housing. Keep the criminal element out, and you'll have less crime. Figures.

Second, they shut the revolving door which had all too often been opened by the Parole Board. Judges would sentence the criminals, all right, but their efforts would be gutted by the Parole Board's leniency. Greenberg began to assign police investigators to appear at the parole hearings, bringing the criminal's victims along! The Board reversed its policy and is no longer soft on victim crimes, particularly burglary, sexual assault, and armed robbery. Guess what? The number of these crimes has dramatically decreased. A simple reality: there will be fewer victims when the criminals are sitting in jail.

Third, the police decided to do their job with truant kids. Realizing they don't ask bankers to approve their arresting of bank robbers, they decided not to ask the school superintendent whether or not they should pick up truants. They just did, and they brought them straight-away to their principals. Daytime crimes decreased by twenty-four percent! And they are serious about curfew at night as well, with similar results.

Fourth, Greenberg initiated a gun-stoppers program, giving a $100 reward for every active gun reported and confiscated. The key word is *active*. Greenberg told about one high school where four students were talking in the restroom, three of them showing off their guns to each other. The fourth student reported it, the police confiscated the guns within minutes, and the reporting student was $300 richer, all accomplished confidentially. A far cry from gun-recovery programs which pay for the turning in of broken and rusty weapons. Talk about getting the "active" guns out of circulation! Why didn't we think of that?

Fifth, the police in Charleston took on the responsibility to eradicate graffiti on private as well as public property. Their graffiti unit removes the stuff the same day it's put on, as often as it happens! Every time! Their clean-up crew works with forty-one different colors of paint.

The chief's talk reminded me of another creative police response. In Boston, when the police realized they were being thwarted often by the requirement for them to have a search warrant in order to enter the quarters of someone on parole, they decided to check up on parolees accompanied by a parole officer who doesn't need a search warrant. Working together, police and parole officer, they have been able to do a much better job with parolees and have reduced their crime rate significantly. If crime can be slowed down elsewhere, why not here?

> *Seek good and not evil,*
>   *that you may live;*
> *And so the LORD,*
>   *the God of hosts,*
>   *will be with you, just as you have said.*
> **Amos 5:14**

# From the Catholic Tradition

*Any human society, if it is to be well-ordered and productive, must lay down as a foundation this principle: that every human being is a person; his nature is endowed with intelligence and free will. By virtue of this, he has rights and duties of his own, flowing directly and simultaneously from his very nature, which are therefore universal, inviolable, and inalienable. If we look upon the dignity of the human person in the light of divinely revealed truth, we cannot help but esteem it far more highly; for men are redeemed by the blood of Jesus Christ, they are by grace the children and friends of God and heirs of eternal glory.*

**Pope John XXIII, *Peace on Earth* (1963), 9–10.**

# For discussion

1. What lessons can you draw from the success stories of this chapter? How do they apply to your local situation?

2. If crime is not being stopped in your neighborhood or your city, why not? Discuss the processes in place, what's working and not working right, steps that must be taken to make your city crime-free.

3. At what point does aggressive crime-stopping become an infringement of personal rights? Are you in imminent danger of crossing that line in your community, your school, your campus? Or is crime-stopping in your situation not aggressive enough?

4. Try rewriting Pope John XXIII's quotation from *Peace on Earth* in simplified language, as one would use with a child. Share your attempt with each other.

# I will advance the concept of the common good

- by participating in or promoting the establishment of a Neighborhood Crime Watch program for our community.

- by promoting gun safety education or a gun-stoppers program in my community, by lobbying for appropriate gun control.

# Personal reflection

# Assets

There is a movement across this nation which is pulling together people of all sorts for the sole purpose of strengthening our neighborhoods and communities, making them healthier environments for our children. The movement is called Healthy Communities and Healthy Youth. Originating here in Minneapolis at an agency called Search Institute, the movement is based on forty developmental assets—positive qualities and characteristics which have proven to be effective in the development of children and youth.

Half of the assets are internal, that is, they exist or should exist in the heart of the young person; qualities like self-esteem, integrity, honesty, responsibility, restraint, sense of purpose, desire to help others, caring about doing well in school, knowing how to plan and make decisions.

The twenty external assets exist or should exist outside the individual. For example, if a child's family provides a high level of love and support, and positive family communication, that child has at least two external assets. But two are not enough. In addition to the positive environment parents provide at home, young people grow well who also have neighbors and other adults who care about them; who have a caring, encouraging school environment; who feel safe at home, in school, and in their neighborhood; who have clear rules and boundaries at home and school and in the neighborhood; who have good role models not only in the adults in their lives but also from their peers; who receive encouragement to do well from their parents and teachers; and who spend at least an hour a week in a religious activity.

Research demonstrates what common sense already knows: namely, that kids grow best in environments that are positive and virtuous and faith-filled. Why is it that promoters of negative, violent, and immoral environments do not listen to common sense but apparently demand that research prove their industries are harmful to kids? For example, both those who produce the violent films, sexually explicit videos, rap music, and other forms of entertainment and their advertisers must be challenged. Greed and exploitation and the absence of a moral backbone, along with a dizzying understanding of the right to free speech may explain why so much of this stuff exists in our society. But these explanations do not excuse. I wonder sometimes whether a class action suit against the purveyors of perversity ought not to be tried to make them pay for the healing and treatment of kids scarred by drugs, violence, and premature sex.

The responsibility to create and maintain a healthy society for the children and youth in our community—this responsibility belongs to every adult. For every adult who exploits and abuses and harms the young, there must be adults who challenge them and call them to accountability.

Parents who are doing their best to raise their children well cannot do it alone. They already have the support of schools and Churches but they need, also, and have a right to the support of other adults in the community, including the entertainment industry, media, and sports world. Yes, it does take a village to raise a child well, because the village—the neighborhood and broader community—are extensions of the "home" to the child.

*My child, do not forget my teaching,*
*    but let your heart keep my commandments;*
*for length of days and years of life*
*    and abundant welfare they will give you.*
**Proverbs 3:1–2**

# From the Catholic Tradition

*Every person is not only sacred, but also social. Human life is life in community. Therefore, the dignity of the individual is inherently connected to the good of society. Human dignity can only be realized and protected in community, and true community is found only where human dignity is respected. The obligation to "love our neighbor" has an individual dimension, but it also requires a broader social commitment. Everyone has an obligation to contribute to the good of the whole society, to the common good. Advancing the common good requires that we respect each person's basic rights and fulfill our responsibilities. Everyone has a fundamental right to life and to those things which make life truly human—food, clothing, housing, health care, education and employment. All have a right to freedom of conscience and religious liberty, to live free from discrimination, and to have a share of earthly goods sufficient for oneself and one's family. People also have complementary duties and responsibilities to one another, to their families, and to the larger society. These duties require all to work for the common good and to respect the rights of others.*

**Archbishop John R. Roach, *Reviving the Common Good*, Pastoral Letter on Social Justice.**

# For discussion

1. Are you willing to wait for scientific evidence that proves, for example, that pornography and violence negatively influence a person's development? Or would you make a claim for common sense? How effective are the entertainment industry's efforts to provide rating systems or systems to screen objectionable material from children?

2. Violent films, sexually explicit videos, and rap music are cited in the chapter as harmful to society. Do you agree or disagree? Explain your thinking and use specific examples to support your position.

3. How do the entertainment industry, media, and sports world promote the common good? How do they influence it negatively? What more could they do to provide a positive influence?

4. Do you agree that those who are childless have an obligation to provide support to parents in their efforts to raise children? If so, what would be appropriate ways for them to provide that support? If not, why not?

5. Of what value are video games? Are there any dangers inherent in the violence which many of them employ to entertain?

6. Parishes and governments use legalized gambling to raise revenues. Do you support this? Why or why not?

# I will communicate for the common good

- by using "I statements" to express myself and by dealing with conflict assertively rather than aggressively.

- by listening to opposing points of view respectfully, making my priority to understand rather than to convince.

- by writing for more information on assets from Search Institute, 700 S. 3rd St., Minneapolis, MN 55415-1138; www.search-institute.org.

# Personal reflection

# A Federal
## *Disaster Area?*

Kudos to the Phillips neighborhood for their move to get their neighborhood declared a federal disaster area! Some of the powers that be do not think they have a chance, but that apparently is not the point. Whether they succeed or not in getting the designation, they have already stated their case with the local officials. Simply put: they're fed up with the guns going off around their children's heads, and the drug-dealing and killing around their homes.

The squeaky wheel gets oiled. For how long and at what decibel must they shout? The mayor said she can't accomplish peace without their help. Are they willing to risk their lives by reporting the gang activity and the gunfire? It takes courage, and the Phillip's folks seem to have it, at least at the moment. Others around town have given up, become discouraged and demoralized. When evil wins, it is because the children of light are too naive to defeat the serpents in their midst. Let me explain.

Some years ago I was invited by the National Guard to tour their operations in Panama as part of a group of citizens from Minnesota. I was impressed with the skills and seriousness of purpose of the men and women representing our nation. They struck me as exemplary humans, devoted and dedicated, and adjusting to a new mission, changing at that time because the Cold War had ended and the threat of world domination by Russian communism no longer existed. Their new mission changed to halting the flow of illegal drugs from South and Central America into the United States.

The more I toured, the more I realized that two very different mind-sets were at work there. Our military personnel, as good as they were, were operating institutionally, that is, they had their jobs, worked their eight hours a day, went to their homes and families after work, spent off-duty hours doing the things average people do. Sure, they wanted to catch the drug-runners and put a dent in the drug trade, and they worked hard while on duty.

But the drug-runners seemed to be working from a totally different motivation. Offer a thug a million bucks if he can get a load into the United States and you're not on a level playing field with civil servants into the eight-hour-work-day-with-no-hassle routine. If the difference is in the passion, the thug has it, and America doesn't have a chance!

Is the same true here at home relative to our community's struggle to stop drugs and the crime that drugs encourage? Do the good guys, the leaders of our government, police, attorney's office, neighborhoods, Churches, and other institutions have the passion needed to match the passion which drives the bad guys? If we don't, we'll never win the war on crime. We need commitment far beyond just putting in one's eight hours. Institutionalized crime-fighting will go only so far in squelching the passion of committed thugs. Unless our institutions can match the motivation of the wily serpents in our midst, our crime and murder rates are not likely to diminish.

So, rise up, Phillips neighborhood! Share your passion with the rest of us!

> *By the blessing of the upright*
>   *a city is exalted,*
> *but it is overthrown*
>   *by the mouth of the wicked.*
>
> **Proverbs 11:11**

# From the Catholic Tradition

*As with any ethical obligation, the participation of all in realizing the common good calls for a continually renewed conversion of the social partners. Fraud and other subterfuges, by which some people evade the constraints of the law and the prescriptions of societal obligation, must be firmly condemned because they are incompatible with the requirements of justice. Much care should be taken to promote institutions that improve the conditions of human life.*

**Catechism of the Catholic Church, #1916.**

# For discussion

1. Define a "movement" and an "institution." Compare and contrast them. Can an effort contain elements of each simultaneously? How . . . or why not? Give examples to support your answer.

2. Think of an administrative bureaucracy with which you are well acquainted, for example, where you work or study. In your estimation does a passion for its mission predominate there? How do institutions stifle passion? What can prevent this?

3. Money is a great motivator for many people. What else can motivate people to action? How can we utilize alternative motivators to promote the common good when our capitalistic economy emphasizes economic motivation?

4. It is said that the only thing necessary for evil to succeed is for good people to do nothing. What is the most serious problem you see in your school or work environment? What efforts of good people would improve this problem situation?

5. Agree or disagree: People use illegal drugs because they lack hope.

6. The *Catechism of the Catholic Church* condemns fraud. How do shoplifting and tax evasion defraud? When might they be defended? How do you respond to an acquaintance who discusses his or her shoplifting or tax evasion?

# I will support enlightened reflection on the common good

- by participating in a round-table discussion or supporting financially a Catholic Worker house in my area.
- by learning about opportunities to support efforts to provide decent low income housing in my area made by Churches and non-profit organizations.

# Personal reflection

# Basic
# *Principles*

A few years ago, Archbishop John Roach published a pastoral letter titled, *Reviving the Common Good.* In it he praised the many people who do good things for the good of society, and he named six of the basic principles most central to the Catholic Church's social doctrine. They are simply summarized:

1. Every human person has a fundamental, God-given sacred dignity. People are more important than things, and must be respected with a reverence that is religious.

2. Every person is not only sacred but is also social, that is, everyone is inherently connected to society and therefore has an obligation to contribute to the common good.

3. Persons have certain fundamental rights, among them, the right to food, clothing, housing, health care, education, and employment. And persons have fundamental responsibilities including the duty to work for the common good and to respect the rights of others.

4. Work is one basic way humans participate in God's creation. Workers have the right to productive work and fair wages, and workers have the duty to put in a conscientious day of work for a day's pay.

5. The common good requires that society assist the weak and vulnerable. "Catholic social teaching suggests that a basic moral test of any society is how the weak are treated." As Christians we are called to respond to all our brothers and sisters, but especially to those who have the greatest needs.

6. We are one human family and are called to solidarity with all people.

Paul's Letter to the Philippians invites us to work for and build up the common good. "Let each of you look not to your own interests, but to the interests of others" (2:4). Christian love continually draws us to care beyond our own limitations and boundaries. Jesus was forever nudging his disciples to care for and nourish the social dimension of relationships. No one of us is an island. We are inseparably interconnected and interdependent.

A current challenge facing our community is that of welfare reform. What began years ago as an institutional response to meet the needs of society's poor has been dismantled at the federal level and now is the responsibility of the states. Archbishop Flynn suggests that, if our current attempt to reform welfare is to result in humane and effective policies and programs, our State legislature must focus on four areas, namely,

1. to invest in job training so those leaving welfare will have an honest chance to become economically self-sufficient
2. to increase funds for child care so parents still raising children are indeed free enough to work
3. to provide an adequate safety net for those who are simply not able to work
4. to protect eligibility for legal immigrants

Every one of us can have an effect on the legislation which is now being shaped. Please consider writing or calling your legislators. Let them know how you feel about the role of government in caring for those in need. Now is the time to act to insure effective and humane welfare reform.

*The rich and the poor have this in common:*
*the LORD is the maker of them all.*
**Proverbs 22:2**

# From the Catholic Tradition

*Government should not replace or destroy smaller communities and individual initiative. Rather it should help them to contribute more effectively to social well-being and supplement their activity when the demands of justice exceed their capacities. This does not mean, however, that the government that governs least governs best. Rather it defines good government intervention as that which truly "helps" other social groups contribute to the common good by directing, urging, restraining, and regulating economic activity. . . .*

**U.S. Bishops, *Economic Justice for All* (1986), 124.**

# For discussion

1. A basic moral test of the strength of any society is how it cares for its weakest and most vulnerable members. Does your community (neighborhood, school, campus, city, state, nation) pass the test? Why do you answer as you do? How well does your community as you define it do in caring for those who are poor in our global community?

2. Welfare reform is a process. At what stage is it now? How must it improve in the future? What would a welfare program which insures adequate compassion include?

3. Christian love urges us to look beyond boundaries, recognizing our interconnectedness. What would Christian love call us toward in matters of the environment?

4. Choose one of the six basic principles of the Catholic Church's social doctrine listed in this chapter. How might an artist illustrate the principle you choose?

5. The text claims that Jesus was forever nudging his disciples to care for and nourish the social dimension of relationships. Find examples of this in the Gospels.

# To develop proponents of the common good, I will

- join Network, the national Catholic social justice lobby. (Information: Network, 801 Pennsylvania Ave. SE, Suite 460, Washington, DC 20003-2167; 202-547-5556; www.igc.apc.org/network.)

- send $15 for Network's Welfare Reform Watcher Packet to both follow and shape welfare reform policy in my state.

# Personal reflection

# Fasting

The Forty Mondays of prayer and fasting are half completed. During the past twenty weeks several parishes, Catholic and Protestant, have joined the over 750 Saint Olaf parishioners who had already committed to pray and fast for the common good of the city and for the building up of the moral fabric of our community. For people who want to do something for the good of Minneapolis, prayer and fasting seems a good way to start. God knows what will come of it all, but surely good will come.

Prayer, fasting, and almsgiving are the three traditional disciplines of Lent. The word *discipline* means teaching, which simply means that as we pray we learn more about our relationship to God, as we fast we learn more about our relationship to ourselves, and as we give alms we learn more about our relationship to others. Of the three, fasting is probably the hardest to do and the most difficult to become habitual. I would like to offer further reflection on fasting.

How often do most Americans really experience hunger? Rarely, I think, because we have so much, and we have so much available to us. There's hardly a moment in our day that we can't put our hands on something to eat or drink. Snacks, fast food, candy, nuts, and a thousand other items are readily handy. Most Americans are habitual grazers from sunrise to sunset and beyond. Refrigerator doors are the most opened doors in our homes. Breaks at work are scheduled every two hours. Next to the car phone are holders for our coffee cups and beverage containers. We rarely feel hunger, and when we do, it's assuaged within minutes.

Fasting makes hunger felt. Fasting is something every Christian is invited to do. It has a remarkably long history in our faith tradition, and for many good reasons. (1) Fasting awakens the heart to the intimate presence of God in one's soul. (2) Fasting encourages more serious reflection about the priorities in our lives. (3) Fasting strengthens our sense of dependence upon God. (4) Fasting sharpens our sensitivity to the spiritual dimension of life. (5) Fasting builds a positive energy against evil. (6) Fasting brings insight into one's own self and one's relation to others. (7) Fasting develops greater appreciation for the gifts of God, especially food and drink. (8) Fasting cleanses a person, spiritually as well as physically.

The prophet Jonah called the entire city of Nineveh to reform its ways. They did, beginning with prayer and fasting, from the king down to the humblest citizen. There was spiritual power in the community's commitment to fast. Fasting is not easy. Fasting is a significant spiritual act. Fasting is a sign of genuine commitment. It's a step or two beyond prayer; it is a kind of prayer, a special kind.

Jesus fasted forty days and forty nights, Scripture says. For the common good of our city, I know that close to a thousand people are fasting for forty Mondays. If you would like to join them, simply make the commitment and join your spirit with the others. Surely good will come of it.

> *Is not this the fast that I choose:*
> *to loose the bonds of injustice,*
> *to undo the thongs of the yoke,*
> *to let the oppressed go free,*
> *and to break every yoke?*
> *Is it not to share your bread with the hungry,*
> *and bring the homeless poor into your house;*
> *when you see the naked, to cover them,*
> *and not to hide yourself from your own kin?*
> **Isaiah 58:6–7**

# From the Catholic Tradition

*In all its activities the Church must seek to preach and act in ways that lead to greater justice for all people. Its ministry cannot neglect the violations of human rights resulting from racism, poverty, poor housing, inadequate education and health care, widespread apathy and indifference, and a lack of freedom. These realities are fundamentally incompatible with our faith, and the Church is required to oppose them.*

**U.S. Bishops, *Statement on American Indians* (1977), 10.**

# For discussion

1. Have you ever attempted to give up a particular food or beverage for Lent? For how long were you successful? What did you learn from that experience?

2. Consider this statement—fasting expands our awareness of the need for healing in society. Do you agree with this statement? If so, how do you think this happens? How do you reconcile the fact that the majority of US citizens are overweight while over 40,000 people worldwide die each day from malnutrition?

3. Consider this statement—fasting is intended to release us from bondage so we can live for God. What enslaves people with whom you interact? From what do you wish to be released, or in other words, what holds you back from your dreams?

4. What good, if any, do you think fasting does in support of the common good of the city?

5. The text lists eight reasons for the long history of fasting in our faith tradition. Rank these reasons from most to least compelling, showing your evaluation of the spiritual reasons to fast.

# I will support the common good

- by fasting, either by myself or with others.
- by eating "lower on the food chain," choosing whole grains and legumes rather than animal protein sources to promote a more equitable sharing of the earth's resources.

# Personal reflection

# A Hub of
## *Hope*

One wall was decorated with proverbs from around the world, another with an urgent message proclaiming that "reading" is a top priority. The hallways and classrooms were neat and clean, the atmosphere serious but upbeat. I was greeted with a hospitable spirit from administrators and faculty; the children were friendly and courteous. This was my first excursion into a Minneapolis public school in years.

Many schools today have had to become full-service agencies, skilled and equipped to do some parenting as well as teaching. With the erosion of family structure, the diminished role of many Churches in building community, the growing numbers of people in poverty, the rising rate of crime, violence, and drug abuse, and other debilitating factors in American society, thank God there remains an institution which still has the possibility of holding a neighborhood together. I do not know what the other public schools are like in Minneapolis. If they are anything like Andersen Elementary in the Phillips neighborhood, they are doing terrific work.

My four-hour visit was filled with inspiring moments: hearing from the schools' leadership of its commitment to human values and seeing the passion for learning among faculty and staff. As for the students, wow, were they beautiful! For a few moments I was allowed to listen in on a mediation session. At a small table were seated four boys, two of whom had gotten into an argument and were required to have their dispute mediated. That's what the other two were doing. Following an outline of steps, the "mediators" worked the disputants toward practical resolutions. This surely beats fists and guns! And it teaches a skill for life.

I had a fascinating hour with a combined class of fifth and sixth graders. The discipline and order within that classroom reminded me of my own parochial school days—hands folded neatly on desks, never once anyone interrupting another while speaking, kids excited to learn. One of the first questions I was asked was: "What would you like us to call you?" "Father John will be fine," I responded. I asked them what their dreams were and what they wanted to be. Their hands flew up! There were two doctors, two veterinarians, a nurse, two teachers, a pilot, an ornithologist, two sports professionals. They showed none of the hopelessness I had thought I would find. This school is doing a terrific job.

When asked what they needed from us to reach their goals, the students listed seven factors, four of which had to do with safety. No more weapons (all but one in the class admitted to hearing gunshots in their neighborhood in recent months), no more drugs or "drive-bys" (shootings), make the world more peaceful, make our streets safe. In addition to safety, they're looking for the community to provide a good education, adequate challenges to spur them on to their goals, and the chance to graduate from college. Well stated!

How can those of us in the Churches help? I asked teachers and principal. They expressed the hope that all Churches work together more to shore up the spiritual and moral bases for families and neighborhood. Help us make our neighborhoods safe. Send us highly skilled professionals who can work with our emotionally disturbed children, and give us more adult volunteers to spend time tutoring and mentoring!

Andersen School in the Phillips neighborhood is more than a symbol of hope for its students. With strong parental involvement and its Family Resource Center, it is also a stimulator of human development for neighbors. A hub of hope; what a gift!

*A gentle tongue is a tree of life,*
*but perverseness in it breaks the spirit.*

**Proverbs 15:4**

# From the Catholic Tradition

*The exercise of solidarity* within each society *is valid when its members recognize one another as persons. Those who are more influential, because they have a greater share of goods and common services, should feel* responsible *for the weaker and be ready to share with them all they possess. Those who are weaker, for their part, in the same spirit of* solidarity, *should not adopt a purely* passive *attitude or one that is* destructive *of the social fabric, but, while claiming their legitimate rights, should do what they can for the good of all. The intermediate groups, in their turn, should not selfishly insist on their particular interests, but respect the interests of others.*

**Pope John Paul II, Encyclical Letter: *On Social Concern*, #39.**

# For discussion

1. The children at Andersen had career aspirations. What are yours? How does or will your career allow you to extend your Christian vocation in the world? In other words, how can you extend the ministry of Jesus as a practitioner of your career or future career?

2. The children of Andersen asked for a safe, nonviolent environment. How safe are the neighborhoods in your community? How weapon-free and drug-free are the schools in your district? How do you promote nonviolence by your personal life choices?

3. The children at Andersen resolved disputes with mediation. Is this option available in your school system or community? Name three personal characteristics which would assist a conflict mediator and tell why you think each characteristic would be important. Who in your discussion group or class would make a good conflict mediator, and why?

4. Relate an incident from your life which illustrates the truth of Proverbs 15:4.

5. How well does or did your educational experience prepare you to promote the common good of society? What factors do or did help or handicap your education toward the common good in school?

6. Consider the quote from Pope John Paul II's letter *On Social Concern* in light of the global distribution of goods. How would a wealthy nation like the United States act in regard to his call? Does the United States seem inclined to share *all* it possesses? In light of Jesus' life, is the pope correct in his statement? As a Christian, how sharing are you of your talents? Your things?

# I will invite consideration of the common good

- by encouraging collaboration between religious groups and other local institutions such as the police force, social service agencies, and the school system.

- by volunteering time in a neighborhood school as a tutor or aide.

# Personal reflection

# Think
# *Common Good*

Reviewing the course of my brief lifetime, six decades now, I believe I have witnessed a major paradigm shift in the driving forces which have shaped our American culture. Perhaps you have, too. The focus back then was strongly on the common good. Pulling out of the great Depression in the 1930s and then winning the Second World War, followed immediately by the need to contain the threat of worldwide communism—these massive events forced Americans to put top priority on what was the best for the community. We really had no other choice than to "get with the program" and work for the good of all.

Then in the late '50s and the '60s, affluence set in, and with it came the variety of options and the focus on the individual. The "we-us-our" focus of my childhood and adolescence days was replaced by the "I-me-mine" paradigm. Never completely, of course, because there have always been prophets and models of community-mindedness. But the forces unleashed by affluence have been strong and the swing toward individualism has been pervasive. Our society has been out of balance ever since. Better balance is not likely to happen without genuine and major efforts to place top priority on the common good.

If companies would ask the common good questions before they downsized, would fewer really have to do it? If corporate raiders would examine their effect on the common good before they bought and stripped down newly acquired subsidiaries, might they have done otherwise? How different would our environment be if common-good issues were faced and dealt with responsibly prior to any exploitation of resources? If stakeholders' as well as stockholders' interests were respected, would the common good be better served?

The good news is that, as a society, we have gotten better at asking common good questions. Environmental legislation is a good case in point of how the brakes can be applied to individual exploitation for the sake of the common good. A whole host of other common good issues are currently being wrestled with: campaign financing, welfare benefits, restriction of televised pornography, education tax credits, suburban sprawl, sex-offender notification, snowmobile driver's licensing, gambling casino taxation, financing an outdoor baseball stadium, to name a few!

Putting a priority on the common good means that the total community's well-being is at least as important as is the well-being of certain individuals. It also means that, for the well-being of the total community, some individuals will have to sacrifice some personal gain. Individual choice is not the highest good.

"Ask not what your country can do for you but rather what you can do for your country" was John F. Kennedy's red flag already signaling in 1960 that the common good was on America's back burner. It's time it be brought to the front.

*If you do good,*
*know to whom you do it,*
*and you will be thanked for your good deeds.*
**Sirach 12:1**

# From the Catholic Tradition

*Such perspectives provide a basis today for what is called the "preferential option for the poor" [A Community of Hope]. Though in the Gospels and in the New Testament as a whole the offer of salvation is extended to all peoples, Jesus takes the side of those most in need, physically and spiritually. The example of Jesus poses a number of challenges to the contemporary Church. It imposes a prophetic mandate to speak for those who have no one to speak for them, to be a defender of the defenseless, who in biblical terms are the poor. It also demands a compassionate vision that enables the Church to see things from the side of the poor and powerless, and to assess lifestyle, policies, and social institutions in terms of their impact on the poor. It summons the Church also to be an instrument in assisting people to experience the liberating power of God in their own lives so that they may respond to the Gospel in freedom and in dignity. Finally, and most radically, it calls for an emptying of self, both individually and corporately, that allows the Church to experience the power of God in the midst of poverty and powerlessness.*

**U.S. Bishops, *Economic Justice for All* (1986), 52.**

# For discussion

1. Explain the perspective called the "preferential option for the poor" as defined in the quote from *Economic Justice for All*. In what ways do you see the Church embody this principle? How does the Church fall short of this ideal? Do you agree with the bishops' statement that Christians need to take the side of the poor?

2. The author relates affluence with individualism. Do you agree? Do deprivation and hardship foster people joining forces? Why do you answer as you do?

3. Choose a common-good issue from the list in paragraph four (top of page 74) to investigate. Consider it in the light of the principle of the preferential option for the poor. State your position as a Christian on the topic you choose.

4. An entertainment industry celebrity advocates the practice of "random acts of kindness": unexpected good acts toward people not personally known by the doer. Does this contradict or foster the spirit of Sirach 12:1? What is an example of a "random act of kindness?" Do random acts of kindness promote the common good or are they merely individual actions?

5. Relate what you have experienced yourself (if over age 60) or learned from listening to someone who lived through the Great Depression, World War II, or the Cold War about prioritizing the common good.

6. Reread the preface of this book. Do you think that the common good is an appropriate starting place from which to tackle the problems of society? Identify some important behaviors which poison society. For each, indicate how individualism approaches this behavior and how a common good approach differs.

# I will actively work for the common good

- by choosing socially responsible funds for my investments.

- by making a personal sacrifice which will promote environmental concern (walking rather than driving, volunteering for highway or park litter clean-up, and so on).

# Common
# *Sense*

## Personal reflection

Parents who protest violence on television are too often told by
free-speech advocates that they need to prove with scientific
certitude that television violence does actually have a negative effect
on children. This proof is hard to come by. Does TV violence hurt
young people? Of course it does; common sense dictates that!

The defenders of violent programming argue, however, that
scientific proof must be obtained to prove the negative effect of the
media on children. Well, proof is nice if you can get it. The reality
is that in many areas of human behavior, scientific proof is not
possible to obtain, perhaps not ever. Consider how long it took
before scientific proof was not only available but accepted relative
to the health risks of smoking. And smoking is easy to prove
because that evidence is physical, concrete, not abstract at all. This
is not so with the effects of the media on the human spirit and
behavior.

There simply are some issues in life that do not subject
themselves to scientific proof. In such instances one can only appeal
to common sense. Common sense, for lack of a more sophisticated
definition, is the "gut-feeling" rational people have about lots of
issues in life, including what's good and what's bad for the next
generation.

Isn't it true that what we eat in our daily diets has an impact,
good or bad, on the quality of our health; that images which flash

regularly on our minds have an impact, good or bad, on our thinking; that the example we see in people we admire influences our moral choices and behaviors, good or bad?

Media producers of all types who fool themselves into thinking they are not doing humanity a disservice by the violence they promote must be confronted by others whose only defense is common sense. The problem has been that the common-sense folk back down all too easily, mistakenly thinking that, well yes, proof is indeed required.

Does violence on television influence human behavior? Forget the demands of the violators of children that proof be given. It can and it does. Insisting on proof for certain issues may be nothing more than an evasion of responsibility. It's time for common sense to prevail.

To press my point: Common sense dictated years ago that repeatedly drawing smoke into a pair of healthy lungs was bound to impair their functioning. But, while the "good guys" were being held at bay for years by self-interest protected by a legal system which doesn't have to operate by common sense, millions of men, women, and children ruined their health.

How long and how many millions of people will it take before common sense dictates and is listened to in areas dealing with the mental and moral health of our society, only one of which is violence on TV? The common good is truly served by common sense.

> By the blessing of the upright
>   a city is exalted,
> but it is overthrown
>   by the mouth of the wicked.

**Proverbs 11:11**

## From the Catholic Tradition

*But these appeals and projects, just as funds privately and publicly allocated, gifts, and loans are not sufficient. For it is not simply a question of eliminating hunger and reducing poverty. It is not enough to combat destitution, urgent and necessary as this is. The point at issue is the establishment of a human society in which everyone, regardless of race, religion, or nationality, can live a truly human life free from bondage imposed by men and the forces of nature that people do not sufficiently control, a society in which freedom is not an empty word, and where Lazarus the poor man can sit at the same table as the rich man.*

**Pope Paul VI, *On the Development of Peoples* (1967), 47.**

# For discussion

1. The author defines common sense as the "gut feeling" rational people have on an issue. How widespread is it, or more to the point: How common is common sense? What prevents people from possessing that sense or from listening to it if they have it?

2. The quotation of Pope Paul VI from *On the Development of Peoples* suggests that violence goes beyond physical battery. How is it a kind of violence when one person or group possesses and uses more than necessary while another person or group is in need?

3. Is smoking sinful? Is it immoral to market cigarettes? Is it evil to promote tobacco use among young people? Defend you opinion.

4. To what extent are you satisfied with media efforts to regulate itself through the use of ratings systems? How effective are these systems in preventing children, youth, and adults from exposure to objectionable material? Why do you think people seek out violence in the media?

5. The author assumes that TV violence hurts young people. Can we assume that violent images harm adults as well? Why or why not?

6. What are other areas beside media violence which could negatively affect the mental and moral health of our society for which credible scientific data may be difficult or impossible to prove?

# I will express commitment to the common good

- by writing to an advertiser to praise or criticize the programming which it supports.

- by participating in/promoting National Turn-Off TV Week (Information: TV Free America, 202-887-0436; www.tvfa.org; tvfa@essential.org), or by turning off the television myself for period of time I determine.

## Personal reflection

# Accountability

My first experience of gross lack of accountability in the workplace was during my college days. For a mere eight days I worked for the city of Saint Paul as a street and alley sweeper. It was my first encounter with major time theft.

My earlier work experience had been the opposite. In grade and high school, I had had several jobs. In my eighth-grade year alone, I had three jobs. I delivered the daily morning and evening papers to over a hundred homes. I stocked, clerked, and home-delivered, on foot, for a local grocery store. In addition on Saturdays and summers, I planted, weeded, hauled dirt, and did whatever needed to be done at a greenhouse. The greenhouse job was my best pay: fifty cents an hour. That was a fair wage for the time, and I earned it, every penny. I began work exactly at 8:00 A.M.; I was given a ten-minute break mid-morning, an hour for lunch, then a repeat for another four hours of uninterrupted work with a ten-minute break in the afternoon. Quitting time was at 5:00 P.M. and not a minute before. The breaks were ten, not even eleven minutes long!

The work habits I learned were good. They paid off in later summers when I worked construction. Commercial builders, these companies made sure they got adequate work out of us for the salaries they were paying. In all my jobs I had always earned the good feeling which comes with honest work.

My experience working for the city was not so. Scheduled to begin at 7:00 A.M., I was always ready to start at 6:45. My first day on the job was the eye opener. Another college student and I waited for more than an hour for our supervisors to finish their card game that they played every morning on company time. It was 9 o'clock before we finally put a shovel and broom to pavement. The half-hour lunch break stretched to nearly two hours to allow time for our supervisors to nap. Three days in a row, when I finished my lunch and was ready to head back to work, I was told by the older men to relax, "just so we're back on the job by 1:00." The afternoon went as the morning: two hours of work for four hours of pay. The taxpayers were getting ripped off, big-time!

My next experience with government was on the federal level. I didn't work directly for Uncle Sam, but as director of a government-funded project, I had to travel several times to the nation's capital to meet with bureaucrats. This experience was not entirely positive. I saw inefficiency institutionalized and incompetence rewarded. In short, there was much to do about nothing, and a lot of bureaucrats, though not officially on welfare, were living off the public coffers.

Happily I have learned since that those two experiences of government were limited. I know plenty of government employees who work hard and are truly dedicated to the good of the people they serve. And I have seen workers employed in private business, especially some of the larger companies, commit theft of time. Accountability is the key. Time theft is wrong no matter in what circumstances it occurs. What happens too easily in big business and big government is the large gap between workers and those they are working for. In business the workers work for bosses. In government the workers really work for the citizens, not for the bureaucracy. The common good is not served well when the gap is huge between those doing the service and those being served.

*Love is patient; love is kind; love is not envious or boastful or arrogant or rude. It does not insist on its own way; it is not irritable or resentful; it does not rejoice in wrongdoing, but rejoices in the truth.*

**1 Corinthians 13:4–6**

# From the Catholic Tradition

*Human dignity also requires the exercise of initiative and responsibility in a society that is free from coercion and inhuman repressions (34). A sound political society will rest on truth when reciprocal rights and duties are recognized in it. Its citizens will be guided by justice, motivated by charity and organized in freedom (35). Human society must concern itself with securing and promoting spiritual values, which will influence all its social and cultural institutions (36). The social order must be a moral one (37), having principles which are universal, absolute, and unchangeable, and having God as the ultimate source of its vitality (38).*

**Pope John XXIII, *Peace on Earth* (1963), 34–38.**

# For discussion

1. Share your own employment experiences of honest work and of time theft. Which is more prevalent in your experience? Why is time-theft morally wrong?

2. To right the wrong of stealing, restitution (paying back) is required. Why is restitution a necessary part of forgiveness of theft?

3. How does time theft affect the common good of a society?

4. To what extent is the employer accountable to the employee? What does a worker have a right to expect from the employer? What happens or what should happen when an employer does not treat the worker fairly? What situations exemplify injustice to the employee?

5. Reflect on Matthew 20:1–16. Jesus' story involving workplace ethics relates to the Church. What point is being made here?

# To deepen our appreciation of the common good, I will

- examine my personal experience of accountability, evaluating it against standards of justice.

- interview an acquaintance about his or her experience of workplace ethics.

# Personal reflection

# The Bottom
# *Line*

Jean-Loup Dherse was CEO of the chunnel project, the underwater link joining London and Paris, a wonder of the modern technological world. He is a former vice-president of the World Bank. His work on world hunger includes authorship of the Vatican's document on that topic.

World hunger—800 million people go to bed hungry every night. The good news about this number is that it is the same as forty years ago when the population of the globe was considerably smaller. So perhaps we have made some progress.

800 million people! An overwhelming number! Even so, Dherse is convinced that individuals can make a difference in spite of the temptation to feel helpless.

Dherse's message is simple gospel. In what we do with our lives, the motivation that will make the difference is Love. Genuine care for people is the answer. Other motivations such as personal gain and institutional advantage are natural and can be good, but we must go one step further. We must ask the "care for people," "the consequences on people" questions. The bottom line must be love. Since those who are poor and hungry are at the end of the line, we must keep probing the consequences of our business and personal decisions, probing their ripple effect down the line, making certain that those who are poor are not affected negatively.

The people in poverty, here and elsewhere around the world, if kept in the equation and given proper consideration, will be the true measure of the morality of our actions. It is individuals, alone or collectively, who shape and pass legislation. It is individuals, alone or collectively, who manage and lead businesses, work on mergers and downsizing, reform health care systems, sustain neighborhoods, administer justice, shape educational institutions, maintain families, determine media quality, and so on.

If poverty is to be eliminated and the structures of society are to benefit the common good, which means all boats rise together, the values of mutual trust and genuine care for people are essential. Every one of us, whatever our state in life, can build trust and love. And we can have a positive effect on world hunger and world poverty by our willingness to sacrifice some personal gain so that the common good can be enhanced.

Immoral practices, anywhere and at any level, destroy trust. Destitution on the one hand and excessive abundance on the other destroy people. Those who are poor have no one to speak for them, and, too often, too few want to listen. The solutions to poverty and hunger are never likely to be perfect or complete, but they will be better if care for people (genuine love) is the bottom line. Only then will the common good truly be accomplished.

We are not drops in the ocean, little as each of us might be. We can make a difference; indeed, we are called by God to make a difference. It is no coincidence that the one commandment Jesus gave us is the command to love God and our neighbor as ourselves.

*We who are strong ought to put up with the failings of the weak, and not to please ourselves. Each of us must please our neighbor for the good purpose of building up the neighbor.*

**Romans 15:1–2**

# From the Catholic Tradition

*In a linked and limited world, our responsibilities to one another cross national and other boundaries. Violent conflict and the denial of dignity and rights of people anywhere on the globe diminish each of us. This emerging theme of solidarity so strongly articulated by Pope John Paul II expresses the core of the Church's concern for world peace, global development, environment, and international human rights. Loving our neighbor has global dimensions in an interdependent world.*

*"For just as the body is one and has many members, and all the members of the body, though many, are one body; so it is with Christ. For in one Spirit we were all baptized into one body—Jews or Greeks, slaves or free . . . If one member suffers, all suffer together with it; if one member is honored, all rejoice together with it. Now you are the body of Christ and individually members of it." (1 Corinthians 12:12–13, 26–27)*

**Archbishop John R. Roach, *Reviving the Common Good*, Pastoral Letter on Social Justice.**

# For discussion

1. What is your thinking about the "difference" an individual can make in improving our society? List some examples of individuals (or jobs) whose decisions have far-reaching impact.

2. If it is true that earth can produce adequate food for the world population, why are 800 million people starving?

3. One Catholic bishop directed his diocese to begin every single meeting of any committee or group by reflecting on the question: How is what we are doing here today assisting the poor?" Why do you think he would ask this? What might result?

4. Working together so that all boats rise together is the principle underlying labor unions. How can unions promote the common good?

5. Without using names, describe someone you know or know of who is poor. Describe the "poorest" place you have ever seen. How could you make a difference?

# I will promote the common good

- by listening to the voices of the oppressed (books, videos, speakers, community meetings, personal conversations).

- by asking myself daily for a week the question "How does what I am doing assist the poor?"

# Personal reflection

# Religion in *Public Life*

On Tuesday, April 28, I participated in the Public Religion Symposium, a gathering of one hundred Minnesota leaders from a variety of professions—the arts, business, media, education, health care, advertising, social services, law, and government. Keynoted by world-renowned theologian, Dr. Martin Marty, the full day of talks and discussion was a fascinating experience. The participants included a few atheists and agnostics intermingled with a variety of believers.

In American society, is religion relegated to the background? Do believers "hold back" from expressing their faith in the public forum? Is organized religion too involved in politics, too public?

I found most interesting a statement attributed to Voltaire and cherished by James Madison. It declared that if a nation has one religion, it would characteristically persecute all others. If it has two, they would war against each other. If it has many, they have to find ways to get along. It was apparent at the Symposium that "getting along" was the goal of the day.

Part of the morning's agenda was working with a "mixed" group. My discussion group included believers of the Hindu, Lutheran, Humanist, Unitarian, Episcopalian, Gospel Church, Jewish, Catholic, and Presbyterian faiths. A negative feeling toward organized religion was palpable from those favoring "spirituality" over "religion." My feeling was that some had been hurt by their Church affiliation and had retreated into privatized faith. An hour was hardly adequate to sort out the variety of feelings, beliefs, and experiences represented in that wonderful mix of people.

In the afternoon we were grouped according to profession. Our task was to arrive at action statements. My clergy group offered two recommendations. First, we need to search together for common moral values and then speak out on issues. Second, we need to consider how morality is eroded when critical religious voices are silenced or indifferent.

The media group called for the inclusion of religion and values in their coverage of stories. They also hoped people could "take their values to work" without proselytizing. Those representing the arts wanted the contemporary art world to consider religious themes as valid forms of artistic expression. They also expressed dismay at what they saw as censorship of art by some religion-based groups.

People in government called for religious institutions to promote the practice of civic engagement and suggested that rules for such engagement be developed (presumably so that proper "separation of church and state" would be maintained). They also were concerned that larger Churches respect non-religionists and minority religions.

Educators called for the teaching about religion in public schools, health care folks wanted medicine to become more holistic, advertisers encouraged the inclusion of spirituality in their field, lawyers acknowledged the necessary tension between religious conviction and the requirements of law in our nation. All in all, it was a good meeting!

As Americans we're getting better at respecting differences among us. A message I came away with was that we need to better identify the common threads of value and faith that hold us together.

*Keep alert, stand firm in your faith, be courageous, be strong. Let all that you do be done in love.*
**1 Corinthians 16:13–14**

# From the Catholic Tradition

*Individuals and groups of citizens must contribute to the common welfare and observe general regulations (53). Civil authorities, likewise, must always act in conformity with present demands of the common good (54). This common good allows for ethnic differences in a group and looks to the true nature of the human person (55). It also requires that all share in it according to their circumstances and without discrimination, though justice and equity may demand special consideration for the less fortunate or the disadvantaged (56).*

*Since the common good affects the whole man, civil authorities must respect the hierarchy of values and foster the individual's material and spiritual commonweal (57–58). Given man's mortal condition, promotion of the common good ought also to include promoting his eternal salvation (59). In general, the common good is served when personal rights and duties are acknowledged and promoted by civil authorities (60). Hence a government not acknowledging or safeguarding the rights of man fails in its duty and lacks authority (61). Its fundamental duty is to regulate society so as to guarantee men's rights and duties or to restore them (62).*

**Pope John XXIII, *Peace on Earth* (1963), 53–66.**

# For discussion

1. What is your experience of religion in the "public square"? Identify places and situations of a public nature where an individual or group expresses religious beliefs.

2. How might religious institutions promote their own engagement in civic affairs without violating the constitutional rights of others? Have religious groups in your experience ever overstepped those bounds?

3. In your community, are there new expressions of religious faith vying with those already established? What makes for good relationships between religious faiths, and between all these believers and their government? What channels exist in your community to facilitate good relationships between religious faiths and between all faiths and their government?

4. What might be an example of a person hurt by organized religion? How do you explain the distinction between "spirituality" and "religion"? How do you explain the distinction between "religion" and "cults"?

5. Choose a religion to investigate. Discover what beliefs and practices differentiate it from others. Investigate a situation of religiously based conflict either from current events or from history to see if it is a case of two primary religions at war with each other, as Voltaire and Madison suggest.

# I will enlarge my vision of the common good

- by visiting a worship service different from my own.
- by voicing a religious perspective on a public issue myself or by encouraging a religious group to do so.
- by lunching with friends at an ethnic restaurant to diversify my tastes.

# Personal reflection

# Ratio
# *Disadvantage*

While assigned to the University of St. Thomas, I lived in a house across the street from the campus. For four years my housemates were another priest and a Christian Brother. We were the basis of our community. Two college students lived in a separate apartment on the third floor. A guestroom on second was occupied occasionally by someone "in need." The ratio of independent, autonomous, untroubled adults in the house was at least four to one.

In time, the other priest in the house moved to a new assignment, and his room became available. To fill it, I had been leaning toward taking in a young man dealing with depression. At the time, a person struggling with an addiction occupied the guestroom. It seemed like a good idea to share the harmonious environment of the house with men hungry for greater stability and emotional nurture in their lives. I talked with my remaining housemate about taking in a second guy in need, and he wisely replied, "No, the ratio won't support it." In his many years as a professional counselor, he had come to believe that the ratio needed to be four to one, that is, four healthy people to support one person carrying major stress.

Recently, in a visit with folks living in one of our city's "war zones," I inquired what their assessment might be of the people who lived there: "What's the proportion of healthy to unhealthy people in this neighborhood?" The response I got shook me up a bit. "Forty percent are involved in crime, maybe fifteen per cent have their lives together and are independent and doing all right, another forty percent or so are on the edge, either physically or mentally or emotionally. It's this last group that often falls prey to the criminals." The ratio in that community apparently was one to seven!

This assessment—granted, it's one person's opinion, and it's a subjective guesstimate—reinforced a theme often expressed by our Catholic Charities office, namely, that the concentration of poverty is such a problem in itself.

The words of Will Steger rang again in my ears. When someone asked him his formula for survival on treks to the North Pole, he said, "I learned that it was critical to surround myself with positive people. One negative person can drag down the whole team." Imagine what happens to a neighborhood when the health ratio is overwhelmingly negative.

So what are law-abiding people to do when surrounded by crime, when their leadership is tired or gives up? Those of us who live in relatively healthy situations need to be reminded about the law of the healthy ratio. One person who's got it together to support seven who are struggling doesn't leave much hope for recovery. The odds are stacked against folks wherever poverty is concentrated. Not only are there insufficient resources to support those in need, but the leadership is so thin, any hope of turning things around is dim at best.

The poor become poorer and hope becomes more distant. The message of the gospel begs for compassionate hearts and selfless service, the kind that stays the course of moral virtue and faces evil head-on with unflagging courage. The sea is so big; the storm so vicious. How can one hope to survive?

*Do not be mismatched with unbelievers. For what partnership is there between righteousness and lawlessness? Or what fellowship is there between light and darkness?*

**2 Corinthians 6:14**

# From the Catholic Tradition

*The very nature of the common good requires that all members of the political community be entitled to share in it, although in different ways according to each one's tasks, merits and circumstances. For this reason, every civil authority must take pains to promote the common good of all without preference for any single citizen or civic group. As Our predecessor of immortal memory, Leo XIII, has said: "The civil power must not serve the advantage of any one individual, or of some few persons, inasmuch as it was established for the common good of all."*

*Considerations of justice and equity, however, can at times demand that those involved in civil government give more attention to the less fortunate members of the community, since they are less able to defend their rights and to assert their legitimate claims.*

**Pope John XXIII, *Peace on Earth* (1963), 56.**

# For discussion

1. Identify the pockets in your community where there are large concentrations of people in poverty. Is the "ratio disadvantage" a reality? Discuss the concept. Learn about the practice of "redlining" neighborhoods. How does it affect the common good?

2. "The message of the gospel begs for compassionate hearts and selfless service, the kind that stays the course of moral virtue and faces evil head-on with unflagging courage." What person you know exemplifies this line from the chapter?

3. An adage states "the poor become poorer." Is this true? Is the reverse true (are the rich becoming richer)? How does Mary's song comment on God's reign with regard to economic disparity (Luke 1:46–55)?

4. What is the meaning of the adage "a rotten apple can spoil the barrel"? How does that saying compare or contrast with the ratio disadvantage concept of four to one?

5. In rural areas, determining the number of homeless people can be difficult since relatives tend to house homeless family members in their own homes. What factors cause people to become or stay homeless? How does a compassionate heart respond to this challenge?

# I will expand my community's understanding of the common good

- by speaking out against the concentration of poverty.
- by helping one person or family escape the downward spiral of concentrated poverty.
- by encouraging persons of wealth to find ways to help people in poverty improve their employment and enjoy greater dignity.

# Personal reflection

# Respect for
# *Authority*

Every time I have gone on a ride-along with the police, I have been deeply impressed by the tremendous courage they must have to do what they do. Their work agendas are very unpredictable. At one moment everything is calm; then in a split second, they are off to an emergency which, more than likely, is bound to be life-threatening. They do not have the luxury of a journalist or a lawyer who can look back on a situation, mull it over for hours, and then determine which response is the best. They have to make decisions on the spot! And quickly!

Since the 1960s, anyone in authority has found the social environment challenging. Parents have been second-guessed by "experts." At times clergy have added criticisms to the parental critique as well. Support for parents who try to fulfill their obligations would more likely be helpful. In schools, teachers and administrators are regularly challenged in the exercise of their authority, not only by outsiders but by students and parents, too. Support for persons in authority would more likely be helpful. It is not easy to be an educator these days, nor a parent.

Nor is it easy to be a police officer. Since the 1960s police have not always received the respect they deserve, and rarely the gratitude and support due them.

I can understand the cynicism that develops when a parent or teacher or priest or police officer abuses his or her authority. Abuse by anyone in authority is unfortunate and wrong. But so is cynicism, the negative attitude that unfairly sustains and encourages disrespect where respect ought to be, and for the common good, needs to be.

In our religious tradition, there are teachings about authority that can serve as a foundation whenever we find ourselves struggling with authority and attitudes toward it. First, all legitimate authority comes from God. As Author of all that is, God is the ultimate source of all authority. Second, everyone who holds rightful authority has received it from God and is ultimately accountable to God for its proper exercise. Third, those rightly subject to authority have an obligation in justice to respect and obey rightful authority, and to appreciate and be grateful to those in authority.

Respect for authority broke down seriously a few decades ago. There were reasons why this occurred at that time. Some reasons are: Watergate, the ambiguity of the war in Vietnam, police brutality in the civil rights struggle, an excessive spirit of individualism. Violations of trust by dishonest persons in the government, betrayals of trust by exploitive teachers, the shattering of faith by sex-abusers among clergy, brutality on the part of police—all these carry an unfortunate after-effect. Trust once broken is difficult to mend and rebuild. Abuse of authority by those in authority leaves scars long after the wounds are healed. But at least when the wounds are healed, the festering has stopped.

Would that it were so with cynicism and the withholding of respect. When people hang on to unfair stereotypes and refuse to let go of impressions which charge all teachers, all clergy, all parents, all police, of misuse of authority when only a handful were actually guilty—such behavior keeps the wounds festering. And the common good suffers as a result.

*Let every person be subject to the governing authorities; for there is no authority except from God, and those authorities that exist have been instituted by God.*

**Romans 13:1**

# From the Catholic Tradition

*The human person is the clearest reflection of God among us. Each person has a special dignity which comes from God. Therefore, every person "must be respected with a reverence that is religious. When we deal with each other, we should do so with the sense of awe that arises in the presence of something holy and sacred." The test of every institution or policy is whether it enhances or threatens human life and human dignity. We must never forget this most basic principle: people are more important than things.*

**Archbishop John R. Roach, *Reviving the Common Good,*
Pastoral Letter on Social Justice.**

# For discussion

1. As you experience the prevailing attitudes toward authority within your community, do you see much cynicism? Withholding of respect?

2. In what ways do you support legitimate authorities? What signs of disrespect do you see in your community?

3. What effect on the common good does abuse of authority have? Right use of authority?

4. How do you think the ability to make good decisions on the spot can be developed? Choose a gift of the Holy Spirit and relate it to this ability which police officers must exercise.

5. Recall a time when you were not treated with respect. Turn it into a story with the moral: "People are more important than things."

6. This chapter suggests several historical events that may have caused a breakdown of respect for authority. Select one and discuss how it may have contributed to such a breakdown. What other events today may negatively influence people's perception of authority figures?

# To strengthen the common good, I will

- send a note of gratitude and appreciation to our local police or to someone else in authority.
- act to lighten the load of my parents. I will call or talk to them with gratitude and love.

# Personal reflection

# Market
# *Driven!*

"The Future of Callings" conference was challenging. About one hundred professionals from ten different professions were invited to think deeply about the impact of the marketplace on their work. There were health professionals, lawyers, clergy, journalists, architects, accountants, law enforcement officers, dentists, engineers, and nurses mulling over present challenges and future possibilities. Some of the signs of the times that emerged were billable hours, bottom line thinking, money's power to corrupt, self-interest over the public's, and "one patient every eleven minutes."

A major theme of the meeting was consideration of the public purpose of the professions. Also discussed were the values that have traditionally inspired the professions. This conference provided a wonderful opportunity for leaders within our community to examine the role of the professions in serving the common good.

No question that the forces of the marketplace have brought about valuable achievements, but, left to themselves, these forces can seriously diminish the quality of life we truly need and want to enjoy. I know people in the medical field, for example, who spend themselves to the point of exhaustion trying to maintain the personal dimension in their profession. After all, medicine is about healing and is an art as well as a science. But third-party payments, managed care and other changes sweeping the medical field are having a powerful impact on how health professionals practice their art.

I know lawyers who feel somewhat betrayed by their calling. Having entered the legal profession for the express purpose of promoting justice in society, they find the pressures of the marketplace impinging upon their integrity and altruism. If the bottom line is money, as the marketplace forces tend to make it, the high road of justice can get terribly blurred.

It was fascinating to hear the architects ponder how frequently function and expediency smother form and beauty in design work these days. Aren't the professions supposed to transcend the forces of materialism?

One of the major presenters at the conference spoke about the positives of money: how it feeds and motivates, connects strangers, mobilizes talent, opens doors, and supplies an element of stability in relationships. He also described the negatives: money vulgarizes, corrupts, distorts, excludes, and is loaded with temptations! So what is money doing to the professions? How is the marketplace changing, for better or for worse, the professions' classic roles, identities, and purpose?

It is of the essence of the professions to serve a public purpose, to exercise public responsibility. This means more than a lawyer or doctor or engineer contributing a certain number of hours of community service. The public purpose of a profession is much more than hours of public service. To do the latter does not adequately substitute for the former, no matter how magnanimous the community service might be.

So how is the marketplace shaping the way we work, the manner in which we live out our "calling" to serve the common good?

*My friends, if anyone is detected in a transgression, you who have received the Spirit should restore such a one in a spirit of gentleness. Take care that you yourselves are not tempted.*
**Galatians 6:1**

# From the Catholic Tradition

*Because we believe in the dignity of the person, we must embrace every chance to help and to liberate, to heal the wounded world as Jesus taught us. Our hands must be the strong but gentle hands of Christ, reaching out in mercy and justice, touching individual persons, but also touching the social conditions that hinder the wholeness which is God's desire for humanity.*

**U.S. Bishops, *Health and Health Care* (1981), 13.**

# For discussion

1. As laudable as it is, the community service done by a professional person (such as tutoring in the local public school) is not likely to fulfill the "public purpose" of the profession (such as a lawyer upholding a high standard of justice). Discuss the difference between volunteer work and professional purpose.

2. What is your assessment of the influence of the marketplace on the professions that touch your life? Are the professionals "selling out" for profit? Why or why not?

3. How does your job or work affect the social well-being of your community? Or: Which of the professions mentioned would most appeal to you? How does it affect the social well-being of your community?

4. Choose one positive and one negative aspect of money mentioned in this chapter to expand upon. In your opinion, which aspect dominates: positive or negative?

5. "Christ has no hands now but yours." Relate an experience you had in which your hands had a positive affect on a person or on a social condition.

# I will engage others in promoting the common good

- by hosting a roundtable discussion centering on the influence of market forces on the professions.
- by utilizing local newspaper, radio, and television opinion forums and talk shows to raise consciousness about the common good.

## Personal reflection

# Enough *Already!*

Every now and then, during my high school teaching days, it became clear to my faculty colleagues and to me that we simply could not meet some of the needs of our students. There were personal and professional needs that were beyond our responsibility as a teaching institution and beyond our capabilities as well. Usually, after considerable discussion, we would have to ask ourselves the "role and responsibility" question: Is this particular need one that is properly ours to respond to? If it wasn't, we had to admit our limitations and say no.

It's amazing to me that schools today can do any teaching at all. More and more, teachers and administrators have taken over the roles and responsibilities of parents. I can't imagine any parent routinely packing a child off to school without providing a nourishing breakfast. But, hey, if kid can eat at school, why not? Physical nourishment like food is easy to supply. Just prepare it, provide it, and no child starves. The schools pick up where homes slack off.

Physical nourishment is one thing; what about emotional? Well, some parents cannot supply this, and others who can, choose other priorities. So here too the schools try to fill the gap, demanding from teachers that they take on more of the home's role.

As if assuming parental responsibilities weren't enough, why not place on schools the responsibility of solving societal issues as well? If kids are using drugs, require a drug education course. If teens are getting pregnant, require sex education. If youth are driving drunk, require driver education. If they're getting obese, require sports and exercise. If neighborhoods are racially unbalanced, use the school system to solve the race problem. If kids with special needs ought to be mainstreamed, use the schools to accomplish this. Real needs, all of these, and good people are trying to do something about them. But is the school the proper vehicle? Can the schools do everything, for everybody, and achieve their own educational purpose as well?

It's no wonder that schools are having trouble teaching the basics! Bless them for what they are able to accomplish. And now comes talk in the state legislature about requiring diversity training. Surely, this is not an evil idea. But are the schools once again being required to respond beyond their proper role and responsibility? Enough already! What will the schools be like a decade from now, given the responsibilities they've taken on beyond the basics of education?

If the schools hadn't been so generous in accepting the multiple roles and responsibilities that home and society have too eagerly dumped on them, might not the test scores look a whole lot better? If, per chance, the schools didn't accept parental responsibilities anymore, and forced them back where they belong, wouldn't teachers and administrators be less distracted from achieving their educational role? If lawmakers and others quit manipulating schools to solve societal problems, would teachers and administrators not accomplish educational objectives and goals better?

No one can do everything, and do it well. For my money, we just might be expecting the schools to measure up far beyond their proper boundaries. But, alas, they must know their own boundaries, too!

> *But we appeal to you, brothers and sisters, to respect those who labor among you, and have charge of you in the Lord and admonish you; esteem them very highly in love because of their work. Be at peace among yourselves.*
> **1 Thessalonians 5:12–13**

# From the Catholic Tradition

*It is a fundamental principle of social philosophy, fixed and unchangeable, that one should not withdraw from individuals and commit to the community what they can accomplish by their own enterprise and industry. So, too, it is an injustice and at the same time a grave evil and a disturbance of right order, to transfer to the larger and higher collectivity functions which can be performed and provided for by lesser and subordinate bodies. Inasmuch as every social activity should, by its very nature, prove a help to members of the body social, it should never destroy or absorb them.*

**Pope Pius XI, *On Reconstructing the Social Order* (1931), 79.**

# For discussion

1. In your own words, what is the main point of this chapter? What is the quotation from Pope Pius XI really saying? Do you agree or disagree with these statements? Defend your answer with reasons.

2. What changes would you make if you were a school superintendent and had the authority to initiate changes?

3. What is the proper role and what are the specific responsibilities of elementary and secondary schools?

4. Teenage drug use, teen pregnancy, drunk driving, racially unbalanced neighborhoods, segregation of those with special needs—choose an issue and brainstorm strategies which don't involve the school system to address the need.

5. Do a school's test scores reflect the economic level of the neighborhood in which the school is located in your town? Explain your observations. In your opinion, how important are standardized test scores?

# I will revitalize the common good

- by gathering representatives of home, school, neighborhood, and Church to review the roles proper to each.
- by examining comparable responsibilities schools have in other developed nations.
- by comparing current school responsibilities with those of fifty years ago, exploring the plusses and minuses of the changes over time.

# Personal reflection

# E Pluribus Unum!

The ancient Greek philosophers wrote about the problem of the "one and the many," and civilizations have been wrestling with it ever since. How does a society achieve a proper balance between the good of individuals and the good of the community?

Every now and then the issue seems to pop up in fresh and contemporary ways. Several years ago, while I was at the University of Saint Thomas, a group of students wanted to establish a new organization in order to promote, protect, and foster their special interest. They felt that their ethnic group was not receiving the respect it deserved. Their "demands" were really nothing more than the respect every human has a right to. So my recommendation to them was to "join the human race" and work together with the rest of the campus on their noble goals—not to give up their uniqueness, but also not to separate themselves from the rest of the student body.

After further reflection, they decided that organizing a special interest group was probably not the best way to respond to their concerns. They recognized a common set of moral values that united them with the larger community.

One hundred and fifty years ago when Father John Ireland was ministering to hordes of new immigrants, he got himself into a major conflict with several other Church leaders. He chose to push for inculturation and inclusion. They wanted the immigrants to keep their native culture, transplanting it from Germany, Poland, and so on onto American soil. Ireland, on the other side of the issue, insisted that the schools teach English, and teach in English in order to "Americanize" the immigrants. His viewpoint won the day, for the most part, and the immigrants learned to blend in and become part of the fabric of a new society.

Many Americans of my generation look back on our immigrant roots. With a tinge of sadness, we feel bad about not knowing "another language," our immigrant parents having chosen to let the old customs and traditions disappear into the background. Our immigrant ancestors had to choose between the dominant American culture and their own roots. Most of them believed that, if their children were going to be successful in America, they had to adapt to the American way of life—not in everything certainly, but at least in using the language of the dominant culture.

Those promoting diversity in our own day are wrestling with this same issue: how to pass along those things which highlight the uniqueness and differences in and among individuals in ways which enhance, but do not impede, inclusion in the dominant society.

Students who come through our educational systems not knowing how to speak English competently will be unnecessarily burdened the rest of their lives. Surely there must be respect for the various cultures and traditions we all represent. But a commitment to the dominant culture requires a certain priority if we are not to impede the futures of our children. As we encourage diversity, let's be sure we are not encouraging separation and alienation.

*For just as the body is one and has many members, and all the members of the body, though many, are one body, so it is with Christ. For in the one Spirit we were all baptized into one body—Jews or Greeks, slaves or free—and we were all made to drink of one Spirit.*

**1 Corinthians 12:12–13**

# From the Catholic Tradition

*Racism is a sin, a sin that divides the human family, blots out the image of God among specific members of that family, and violates the fundamental human dignity of those called to be children of the same Father. Racism is the sin that says that some human beings are inherently superior and others essentially inferior because of race. It is the sin that makes racial characteristics the determining factor for the exercise of human rights. It mocks the words of Jesus: "Treat others the way you would have them treat you." Indeed, racism is more than a disregard for the words of Jesus; it is a denial of the truth of the dignity of each human being revealed by the mystery of the Incarnation.*

**U.S. Bishops, *Brothers and Sisters to Us* (1979), 9.**

# For discussion

1. *E pluribus unum* means "one from many." What are the diversity issues confronting your community? Identify the points of separation, the points of unity, for each issue.

2. Is it possible to have both diversity and unity at the same time? Discuss. How does this relate to the common good?

3. Several states in the United States have declared English as their official state language. What are the ramifications of this? What are the advantages and disadvantages of programs which teach English as a second language in our U.S. schools?

4. What are the corporal and spiritual works of mercy? In your opinion, which one most appropriately relates to the content of this chapter? Why?

5. What are the special needs of immigrants? Does the Church have a responsibility to minister to immigrants differently than it does to those of the dominant culture? Is there a specific ministry to immigrants in your diocese? If so, of what does it consist?

# I will explore common good issues related to immigration

- by interviewing recent immigrants to learn how they are experiencing inclusion and exclusion.

- by reading up on the histories of immigrant groups in the U. S., comparing the past with the present.

- by developing a friendship or by sharing with a recent immigrant or immigrant family.

# Personal reflection

# Values in *Public Schools,* Part 1

It was the most anxiety-riddled day of my life. Neither before nor since have I experienced my neck as knotted or a headache so painful. For six and one-half hours, I was the subject of a legal deposition, being questioned under oath. The year was 1984!

With me in the room were six lawyers and a court recorder. The two New York lawyers from the ACLU, the American Civil Liberties Union, were determined to prove that I had violated the separation of church and state. The other four were on my side: two from the U.S. Department of Justice to protect the government, the remaining two hired by Search Institute to protect my rights and Search's. You see, as director of a sexuality curriculum project funded by the federal government, I was suspected, most likely because I was a priest, of trying to teach religion in the public schools.

What made my involvement even more suspicious was our curriculum's explicit promotion of values, seven of them: *equality, honesty, promise-keeping, respect, responsibility, self-control,* and *social justice.*

Values! Whoever convinced the public education establishment that instilling values was a violation of the separation of church and state perpetuated one of the greatest hoaxes of this century. The belief that public schools should not teach values is patently false. For one thing, it's impossible to not teach values. The real question is which values.

Back in 1984, when our curriculum team from Search Institute was piloting our values-based material, most of the public school administrators and teachers in the project initially questioned our inclusion of values. They had bought the line that their schools had to be value-free. But as our training sessions progressed and they began to teach the curriculum, they realized they could, indeed should, teach values in their schools. Indeed, within five years time, over 2,000 public school districts nationally had adopted this curriculum!

It was reassuring, a few weeks ago, to hear the Minneapolis Superintendent of Schools note that the public schools used to think they were not supposed to teach values. "Of course we can," she continued. "There are universal values, common to all people." Then she listed three: honesty, caring, and responsibility. I wanted to shout: "Amen! Right on!" I agree, provided "teaching" values also means "instilling" them. I'll say more on that in the next session.

Oh, by the way, the ACLU eventually dropped us from the lawsuit!

*So then, putting away falsehood, let all of us speak the truth to our neighbors, for we are members of one another.*
**Ephesians 4:25**

# From the Catholic Tradition

*Development which is merely economic is incapable of setting man free; on the contrary, it will end by enslaving him further. Development that does not include the* cultural, transcendent and religious dimensions *of man and society, to the extent that it does not recognize the existence of such dimensions and does not endeavor to direct its goals and priorities toward the same, is* even less *conducive to authentic liberation. Human beings are totally free only when they are completely* themselves, *in the fullness of their rights and duties. The same can be said about society as a whole.*

**Pope John XXIII, *Peace on Earth* (1963), 88.**

# For discussion

1. Develop a workable definition for each of the seven values listed above. Why is it that we can correctly term these "moral values?"

2. Moral values have to do with right and wrong. How is it not only appropriate but also essential that basic moral values be taught in public schools?

3. Draw up a listing of issues, problems, and crises that face us in our contemporary world. From the seven values highlighted in this chapter, assign to each contemporary challenge values which are necessary in order to address that challenge.

4. Recall and share an experience from your own education in which one of the seven values listed in this chapter was incorporated into the curriculum. If you are unable to remember such an experience, reflect on the importance of that reality. Choose one of these values and develop a lesson plan of how you might teach that value to a group of younger children.

5. Reflect on behavior you have seen or of which you are aware in your neighborhood, in your workplace, in your school system, in any public arena. Consider the values highlighted in this chapter. How were they present or absent in that behavior? How did the incident affect you personally? How do you regard the individual responsible for the behavior?

# For the common good, I will enhance my public school's civic role

- by encouraging the school's promotion of character formation or by teaching a mini lesson on values to a small group of students in public or religious education.

- by facilitating the school board's formal adoption of a universal set of moral values.

- by sponsoring teacher and parent inservice on the moral values of the community.

## Personal reflection

# Values in
## *Public Schools,*
### Part 2

Values are not taught, but "caught." *Knowing* what is right and *doing* what is right are not the same! The ancient Greek philosophers realized that knowledge and virtue are indeed two different things. Did we forget?

Teaching universal values such as honesty, caring, and responsibility—to list the three suggested by the Minneapolis Superintendent of Schools—is very different from "instilling" values, that is, sinking moral convictions deep into the hearts of anyone. For discussion sake, I would like to offer five elements that I believe are essential if our children are to grow morally.

But, first, let's begin with a word about the term *moral*. For those in the public school system or elsewhere who equate moral with religious, think a moment. Is it a wrongdoing or not if a thief gains access to your bank account and steals your life-savings? That's stealing, pure and simple. It's a moral wrong. I have been in secular settings where the word *moral* has been dumped because, to some, it sounds religious, so they think they must ban the word from the public square. Give the word a break!

Should the public schools be teaching morality? Yes, yes, yes! And, in doing so, they do not infringe on constitutional separation of church and state.

Five basic elements in the process of building ethical, moral persons are: (1) positive role models, (2) positive peer influence, (3) effective sanctions, (4) support from subgroups and larger community, and (5) personal acceptance of a moral authority outside oneself.

If children know that honesty, caring, and responsibility are cherished *and lived* by the significant adults in their lives, they have a good start toward becoming morally good themselves. When their peer group, especially the real leaders among them, also holds these values, they are strengthened in their efforts to be honest, caring, and responsible. Being human, young people will learn to act morally often because not to do so will simply result in a negative consequence. So sanctions are an important and positive element in moral development. Furthermore, since most kids do not live in glass bubbles; their efforts to be moral need the support of their neighborhood communities and the other groups they belong to. Finally, without a moral authority to whom one is accountable (God, Allah, a Higher Power, even the common good of society), morality is a self-deception.

One becomes honest, caring, and responsible by BEING honest, caring, and responsible, time after time, day after day. It's time to recommit to moral development, a process that is not all that complicated. Five basic elements! But do not leave any one of them out. And do not think, for a minute, that teaching ABOUT moral values is enough to INSTILL them. (Good going, Superintendent! But don't tell anyone a priest supports your efforts. Separation of church and state, you know!)

*Remind them to be subject to rulers and authorities, to be obedient, to be ready for every good work, to speak evil of no one, to avoid quarreling, to be gentle, and to show every courtesy to everyone.*

**Titus 3:1–2**

# From the Catholic Tradition

*The conviction that all men are equal by reason of their natural dignity has been generally accepted. Hence, racial discrimination can in no way be justified, at least doctrinally or in theory. And this is of fundamental importance and significance for the formation of human society according to those principles which We have outlined above. For, if a man becomes conscious of his rights, he must become equally aware of his duties. Thus, he who possesses certain rights has likewise the duty to claim those rights as marks of his dignity, while all others have the obligation to acknowledge those rights and respect them.*

**Pope John XXIII, *Peace on Earth* (1963), 44.**

# For discussion

1. Explore the difference between knowledge and virtue, between knowing what is right and doing what is right. What factors block putting knowledge of correct behavior into action?

2. What is the goal of our country's school system? Would you agree that all schools (public and private, K through 12) have the responsibility to promote a basic ethical and moral development in their students? This goes beyond information for the mind to formation of character. How is this so?

3. Why is it important, indeed critical, for the home, neighborhood, religious organizations, and community at large to be in sync with the school on character formation?

4. Pope John Paul XXIII's statement indicates that every right carries with it a corresponding obligation. Using the United Nation's Universal Declaration of Human Rights (1948), draw up a list of human responsibilities that correspond to those rights. Visit the Web-site of the United Nations High Commissioner for Human Rights at www.unhchr.ch.

5. Elaborate on the five basic elements in the process of developing moral persons by choosing an element and expanding on its importance. Tell how you think the community, religious organizations, neighborhood, and family can strengthen or support the element you select.

## To review the common good of our community, I will

- focus community attention on a set of common moral values.
- plan with others how to promote morality without being moralistic in approach (such as by producing and distributing pocket-sized cards reminding citizens of the community's moral standards).

## Personal reflection

# Universal
# *Moral Values*

The word *values* refers to the set of principles and standards which individuals and communities use to guide their decisions and behaviors. Moral values are those principles and standards having to do with right and wrong, with moral and immoral activity. A good example is the moral value of honesty which, when adhered to, supports people in truth telling and helps them avoid behaviors such as stealing and lying.

For people of religious faith, universal moral values are often understood in light of their religious beliefs. For example, when persons of religious faith steal something, they are likely to consider stealing to be a sin, that is, a turning one's back on God, as well as a moral wrong. For them, the religious dimension adds an important aspect of meaning to universal moral values. With or without the context of religious faith, universal moral values serve as a valid compass for right and wrong. They transcend religious, political, socioeconomic status, and ethnic or racial divisions. Reasoning and reflective persons have aspired to them from time immemorial.

Is there a list of universal moral values? Surely, and more than just one list. Since these values are of an intangible nature and somewhat subjective, they can be considered variously. The listing I would like to support is the following:

1. **Respect.** Treating self and others with reverence in every way; respecting the person and property of self and others, including personal reputation; avoiding substances and

actions harmful to physical, moral, and spiritual health; having reverence toward nature and the environment.

2. **Trustworthiness.** Being honest; acting with integrity; trusting others and being worthy of trust; being faithful to promises made and obligations assumed.

3. **Responsibility.** Fulfilling duties and obligations toward family, friends, workplace, school, religious community and civic community; commitment to the common good of society.

4. **Fairness.** Acting justly toward others; acknowledging equality among all peoples; being reasonable in expectations placed on others.

5. **Caring.** Being considerate of others, compassionate and kind toward all, especially those in need; observing common social courtesies.

These moral values are universal. They apply to human activity of all kinds whether in the home, at work, in business or government, the public forum, public and private school classrooms, for-profit and non-profit boardrooms, restaurants and shopping malls, sports arenas and entertainment halls, the media and, indeed, wherever humans meet. Societies thrive when individuals not only accept these values as ideals to be striven for, but hold one another accountable to act accordingly. Although ideals are never fully realized, their role is nonetheless essential in establishing and maintaining healthy human communities.

> *Rid yourselves, therefore, of all malice, and all guile, insincerity, envy, and all slander.*
>
> **1 Peter 2:1**

# From the Catholic Tradition

*Permit me to enumerate some of the most important human rights that are universally recognized: the right to life, liberty and security of person; the right to food, clothing, housing, sufficient health care, rest and leisure; the right to freedom of expression, education and culture; the right to freedom of thought, conscience and religion; and the right to manifest one's religion either individually or in community, in public or in private; the right to choose a state of life, to found a family and to enjoy all conditions necessary for family life; the right to property and work, to adequate working conditions and a just wage; the right of assembly and association; the right to freedom of movement, to internal and external migration; the right to nationality and residence; the right to political participation and the right to participate in the free choice of the political system of the people to which one belongs.*

**Pope John Paul II, *Address at the United Nations* (1979), 13.**

# For discussion

1. What do you think about the list of five universal moral values offered in this essay? What would you add that could not fit under those listed?

2. Study the five values as defined, then discuss how well they reflect the good of individuals and the good of the broader community.

3. Discuss the universality of these moral values. Would they be accepted around the globe? In your workplace, neighborhood, shopping mall, and so on?

4. Consider Pope John Paul II's list of human rights in the above statement. Is what situations in the world today are some of these human rights unjustly denied?

5. Select an autobiography or biography of a respected person. Find examples of the universal moral values given in this chapter as evidenced in his or her behavior. Look for adversity in that person's life that was caused by immoral behavior or by the absence of one or more human rights. How did he or she deal with the adversity?

# For the common good, I will build up the moral fiber of my community

- by selecting one moral value upon which to concentrate this week and reviewing daily how I incorporated it into my actions.
- by speaking up for moral values in a situation of injustice in my local community or in our global community.

# Personal reflection

# Moral Values
## *and Religious Faith*

In discussions about whether or not public schools may teach moral values, an important distinction must not be lost. Opponents' voices tend to insist that to teach moral values in public schools is to teach religion and therefore a violation of the separation of church and state. Though this is not the case, their perspective has held sway in recent decades but, thankfully, is being reevaluated.

Values talk can be threatening since values touch the deeply personal in life, and they do, in people of religious faith, become intertwined with the religious dimension. Values talk can be confusing, too, because of its complexity. Values come in various shapes and sizes, but simply put, a value is something of worth. Some values are personal—an heirloom or treasured family photo. Some values are social: friendship, or a sense of community in a neighborhood or church. Some values are common aspirations of practically all humans. Some examples are a world at peace, a caring family, personal freedom, human equality, beauty, wisdom, and happiness.

Some values are distinctly moral, having to do with right and wrong. For example, people with religious faith may believe strongly that, if peace and happiness are to be achieved in a school or community, individuals must treat each other with respect. They must also respect each other's property and must act in caring ways toward each other. Violent behaviors, stealing, lying, cheating, are disrespectful and morally wrong.

In a school setting, it is unethical (wrong) for anyone to deliberately and knowingly disturb the learning environment by behaviors which infringe upon the rights of other students to learn and teachers to be obeyed. The rights of students to receive an education and the responsibility of students to obey their teachers go hand in hand! Several moral values are involved here: respect, courtesy, self-control, and obedience—all necessary if the human value of a quality education is to be achieved. Religious faith adds to this setting a perspective that includes the believer's relationship with the Divine. A student who believes in God may very well be motivated to behave in class because to do so is to honor and please one's God.

To people of a religious faith—let's use the Christian faith as an example—morally wrong behaviors are seen as more than simply moral wrongs; they are sins. *Sin* is a faith word. It arises out of a view of the world that believes that God is the one who calls humans to act rightly. Not only has God given humans the capacity to choose, and therefore to love, but God calls humans to choose rightly and love tenderly. Such a relationship implies not only the possibility of love between God and humans but also the challenge for humans to act with love for one another.

To persons of the Christian faith, moral wrongs are seen as disobedience toward God. Immoral activity is a turning of one's back on God who loves us, gives us everything we have, and calls us to live lives of moral goodness. To do what is good and to avoid evil is the basic imperative. To comply with this basic imperative is, at least, to begin to love. It's this relationship between the person of faith and God that is the religious dimension of value talk.

So, what's a public school to do about teaching moral values? Teach, and not only teach them, but form them as well in the character of the student. This is the minimum that public education must do. And public education can do more. It can recognize that vast numbers of people have religious faith. Without violating the constitution, schools can show respect for religion and even include discussions about religion in the curriculum.

*I know what it is to have little, and I know what it is to have plenty. In any and all circumstances I have learned the secret of being well-fed and of going hungry, of having plenty and of being in need. I can do all things through him who strengthens me.*

**Philippians 4:12–13**

# From the Catholic Tradition

*Private ownership confers on no one a supreme and uncon-
ditional right. No one is allowed to set aside solely for his
own advantage possessions which exceed his needs when
others lack the necessities of life.*

**Pope Paul VI,** *On the Development of Peoples* **(1967), 23.**

*Christian tradition has never upheld this right [to ownership]
as absolute and untouchable. On the contrary, it has always
understood this right within the broader context of the right
common to all to use the goods of the whole of creation: The
right to private property is subordinated to the right to
common use, to the fact that goods are meant for everyone.*

**Pope John Paul II,** *On Human Work* **(1981), 14.**

*No one can ever own capital resources absolutely or control
their use without regard for others and society as a whole. This
applies first of all to land and natural resources. Short-term
profits reaped at the cost of depletion of natural resources or the
pollution of the environment violate this trust.*

**U.S. Bishops,** *Economic Justice For All* **(1986), 112.**

# For discussion

1. From the essay, list various values. Think of an example not
   mentioned in the text for each type of values. How are
   moral values distinct from all the other types mentioned?

2. Explore the added dimension which religious faith gives to
   moral values. To do this, choose a value such as honesty,
   reverence toward life and the environment, compassion
   toward people in need. Discuss how faith enhances or deep-
   ens the meaning of the moral value you choose.

3. List some behaviors of either students or workers that you
   think are morally wrong without being criminal or against
   civil law. How should this type of immoral behavior be
   handled by school administration or by labor management?
   Use the experience of yourself or others to support your
   answer.

4. The quotations from the Catholic Tradition section of this chapter are about Catholic teaching on the concept of private property. Restate each quotation in your own words. When is private property immoral? In the light of this chapter, how would a person of Christian faith explain this teaching on private property?

5. When would a people of religious faith consider pollution or the depletion of natural resources sinful? Why does a person of faith consider this moral wrong to be evil? Give examples of human behaviors that counteract pollution or depletion of resources. How might a person of religious faith name or describe behaviors that are the opposite of sinful?

6. Using this chapter as a basis, explain how it could be morally wrong to neglect to vote in a public election. In your opinion, could it be sinful to neglect to vote?

## I will add the spiritual dimension to the common good

- by identifying from my faith tradition the beliefs which undergird for me the five universal values identified in the previous chapter.

- by composing five prayers, one for each of the universal values, which set each value in a religious context or by preparing an invocation on universal moral values which someone could use at a public school graduation.

## Personal reflection

# Where's *the Baby?*

Throw out the baby with the bath water! Those of us old enough to remember the "olden days" before the revolution of the 1960s were taught a moral code which found no embarrassment at all in using the word *should.* And the word *ought* was there right next to it.

*Ought* and *should.* Two words that had the wind kicked out of their sails during the "enlightened" era of the 1960s, some of it justified. Yes, the "olden days" did over-emphasize the law rather than the spirit at times. Yes, there were many of us who followed the rules because we believed we should have. Deep in our bellies there was a sense of "oughtness" about certain behaviors, either we ought NOT or we ought TO act in a particular way.

Then came the revolution. Suddenly it seemed all the old rules came under fire. Not only that. The very use of the words *ought* and *should* became socially incorrect. People who used such language were considered hopelessly out of date and accused of malforming the consciences of the young, as well as plunging their self-esteem to the depths. Along with *ought* and *should,* out the door went the word *wrong.* (This was about the time that the word *sin* was also banned from conversation.)

Stealing, maiming, lying, cursing, and such became known as "inappropriate," according to the new leaders of the revolution. Political correctness of the day forbade anyone to accuse another of doing "wrong." Behaviors, which for centuries were accurately labeled WRONG, suddenly became whitewashed as "inappropriate." Give the world a break!

Moral wrong by any other name is still moral wrong. Chewing gum in class may be inappropriate; stealing is wrong. Some of us grew up at a time when the top seven public school problems were: talking out of turn, chewing gum in class, making noise, running in the halls, cutting in line, dress code infractions, and littering. All certainly inappropriate behaviors, impolite even. Forty years later the same CBS poll resulted in quite a different list: drug abuse, alcohol abuse, pregnancy, suicide, rape, robbery, and assault. Inappropriateness doesn't begin to address the moral content of these behaviors.

Back-to-the-basics of morality will require a return to an accurate use of the words *should* and *ought*. It will also require the concurrent recognition that, for our own good, we need to recover the moral language of right and wrong. At the same time, we must recognize that "printed on our hearts" by the Creator is the truth of moral obligation. There are moral rights and wrongs, and yes, there are also inappropriate behaviors. Equating the two, however, leaves us afloat on stormy seas with neither compass nor rudder.

We see the bath water all around us. Where's the baby?

*Finally, all of you, have unity of spirit, sympathy, love for one another, a tender heart, and a humble mind. Do not repay evil for evil or abuse for abuse; but, on the contrary, repay with a blessing. It is for this that you were called —that you might inherit a blessing.*

**1 Peter 3:8–9**

# From the Catholic Tradition

*The church has the right, indeed the duty, to proclaim justice on the social, national, and international level, and to denounce instances of injustice, when the fundamental rights of man and his very salvation demand it. The Church, indeed, is not alone responsible for justice in the world; however, she has a proper and specific responsibility which is identified with her mission of giving witness before the world of the need for love and justice contained in the gospel message, a witness to be carried out in Church institutions themselves and in the lives of Christians.*

**Synod of Bishops, *Justice in the World* (1971), 36.**

# For discussion

1. What's meant by the expression "to throw out the baby with the bath water"? In the context of this chapter, what is "the bath water" and what is "the baby"? Do you agree or disagree with the author's viewpoint? Share what you think.

2. Do you believe there is a basic sense of moral obligation "imprinted" on the hearts of humans? What evidence do you have to support your belief?

3. Share your experience with conversations about moral behavior: Do you ever find the words *should* and *ought* banned? Why do some people object to the use of these words? Is *inappropriate* substituted for *wrong*? Why do some people make this substitution? Explore the potential consequences of both styles of conversation with regard to the morality of human behavior.

4. Read Matthew 7:1–5. How is the Church's duty to proclaim justice as quoted above from the bishops' synod reconcilable with a prohibition on judging others?

5. What is meant by the term *politically correct?* What are examples of political correctness? Why do some people object to the idea? Where is the morality in this controversy? How does it relate to the common good?

# For the common good, I will examine the quality of my community's moral strength

- by gathering anecdotal information on how safe senior citizens feel today compared with their feelings thirty or forty years ago.

- by conversing with my Church's "elders" about what they believe to be the basic foundations of morality.

- by encouraging young people to lead by example.

## Personal reflection

# Historical
## *Perspective*

How do we define the phrase *the common good?* It is best defined as the sum total of those conditions of social living whereby people are enabled more fully and more readily to achieve their God-given purpose. Two pillars support the notion of the common good. They are (1) respect for the inviolable dignity of every human, and (2) a recognition of the social, thus interdependent, nature of humans.

The principle of the common good is a dynamic one. Thus it must be applied by every generation to changing times. Humans are, by nature, social beings. Even so, the individual is the foundation of every social institution. Put simply: The good of the individual person and the good of society are two counterbalancing goods. Both are essential for humankind's fulfillment.

Plato and Aristotle believed that the common good of society was served by individuals acting virtuously and by government providing a stable environment for its citizens. Later, Augustine taught that the common good of society was peace. For him that meant an ordered harmony among citizens themselves as well as between the government and the people. Thomas Aquinas wrote about the common good in terms of people living well together, living the good life. The good life, he taught, was the virtuous life. For him, basic to living the good life were (1) protection from enemies and (2) the attainment of the basic necessities of life.

Aquinas also taught that it was not possible for a person to be truly good unless that person was also well ordered to the common good. In other words, every individual must respect the requirements of the broader society. *The Catholic Encyclopedia* notes that for Aquinas "the common good of the state cannot flourish, unless the citizens be virtuous, at least those whose business it is to govern. But it is enough for the good of the community that the other citizens be so far virtuous that they obey the commands of their rulers."

Over the centuries, discussion about the common good has wrestled with the two pillars of (1) rights and responsibilities of the individual and (2) the rights and responsibilities of society. For centuries, the common good of society held a certain priority over the individual good. The Enlightenment changed all that as philosophers pushed the notion that individual good was, in effect, the common good. This favored individuals who had the wherewithal to get on top and stay on top. Not surprisingly, those who were poor were left out of this equation.

In 1891, Pope Leo XIII initiated a century of serious reflection and emphasis on the good of society, while retaining a profound respect for the inviolable dignity of the individual. Catholic social teaching has consistently called governments to care for the common good. It calls governments to insure the dignity of persons while establishing and maintaining a social environment that benefits all. In short, the individual's role is to obey the just requirements of government. The government's role is to promote social living that assists individuals so they can achieve their God-given purpose, both as individuals and as social beings.

*To each is given the manifestation of the Spirit for the common good.*

**1 Corinthians 12:7**

# From the Catholic Tradition

*In its teaching, the Church has noted a number of basic human rights in economic life, including the right to productive employment, the right to just wages, the right to an adequate income, the rights of workers to organize and bargain collectively, the right to own property for the many as a protection of freedom, and the right to participation in economic decisions.*

**U.S. Bishops, *To Do the Work of Justice* (1978), 28.**

# For discussion

1. Economic systems affect the common good. Explore the ways capitalism thwarts or develops the common good. Explore the ways socialism promotes or detracts from the common good.

2. Imagine situations of imbalance: In one situation the individual good is exaggerated, in another the good of society is exaggerated. The analogy, "all boats rise together," may help your discussion stay practical. Try to use local situations familiar to you.

3. Discuss a current legislative issue in which the government, as represented by the legislators, is wrestling with the balance between the individual's and society's good. For instance, in the case of legislation requiring motorcycle operators to wear helmets, how do individual's rights and society's good intersect?

4. How do you define these terms: the common good, the good life, peace, a virtuous individual?

# I will develop a timeline on the common good

- by charting the evolution of the concept of the common good from Plato to John Paul II.
- by developing a future timeline suggesting global common good goals for the twenty-first century.

## Personal reflection

# The Code
## *of Silence*

What is the common good? It's a principle of moral and ethical behavior that too often gets short shrift in our individually oriented and self-focused society. My first unforgettable lesson on this principle was in high school.

A student had stolen the master key that opened student lockers and regularly would burglarize someone's belongings, usually pilfering valuables and money. As time went on, an atmosphere of distrust and fear swelled throughout the student body. Then, one day at an all-school assembly, the principal described how this student's behavior was negatively affecting the whole community. Then he played the common good card, telling us that this was not the time to keep a "code of silence." In other words, if any of us knew who the culprit was, we had a moral obligation to urge the guilty one to confess, and if he refused, to inform the authorities ourselves, before even greater damage occurred.

The principle of the common good applies at many levels of human activity. Opponents of land mines, chemical weapons, pollution, and global warming take the principle of the common good seriously. Those who are cleaning up "brownfields," halting drug traffic, or working to stop abortion and assisted suicide, are acting for the welfare of the broader society. They realize that the behaviors of some can have a powerfully negative impact on large portions of the human family. Thus, for the common good of all, they are willing to give of their time, energy, and resources.

The depletion of the ozone is a case which is clear and to the point. If the principle of the common good had been more actively applied during the industrial revolution and the last 80 years of carbon-monoxide-spewing automobiles, we wouldn't be pondering the potential flooding of our coastal cities.

Closer to home, shouldn't the principle of the common good be given more consideration in discussions about suburban sprawl, affordable housing, "war-zone" neighborhoods, sentencing guidelines, high school drop-out rates, racism, and concentrated poverty? These issues for sure involve the common good, and others do also: the AIDS epidemic, teen pregnancy, divorce, and child abuse, to mention some.

Simply put: The principal was right on when he forced us to consider the broader moral ramifications of one culprit's activity and the additional harm being done by others of us wrong-headedly shackled by the "code of silence." Moral issues are often societal and even global in influence. Therefore, we must include in our moral reflection the impact of individual behaviors upon the broader social body. The good of the individual and the good of the community (family, team, neighborhood, city, state, nation, global community) are co-essential pillars of morality. They are interdependent. If one is neglected, the other is weakened as well.

The principle of the common good is not a static one. It is dynamic, always in need of application as situations change and life moves on. If this principle is ignored or given only minimal consideration, the results can be detrimental to all.

*Let love be genuine; hate what is evil, hold fast to what is good; love one another with mutual affection; outdo one another in showing honor.*

**Romans 12:9–10**

# From the Catholic Tradition

*We maintain that abolition of the death penalty would pro-*
*mote values that are important to us as citizens and as*
*Christians. First, abolition sends a message that we can*
*break the cycle of violence, that we need not take life for life,*
*that we can envisage more humane and more hopeful and*
*effective responses to the growth of violent crime . . . .*
*Second, abolition of capital punishment is also a manifes-*
*tation of our belief in the unique worth and dignity of each*
*person from the moment of conception, a creature made in*
*the image and likeness of God . . . . Third, abolition of the*
*death penalty is further testimony to our conviction, a con-*
*viction which we share with the Judaic and Islamic tradi-*
*tions, that God is indeed the Lord of life . . . . Fourth, we*
*believe that abolition of the death penalty is most consonant*
*with the example of Jesus, who both taught and practiced*
*the forgiveness of injustice.*

**U.S. Bishops,** *Statement on Capital Punishment* **(1980), 10–13.**

# For discussion

1. Is there a "code of silence" in your world: at work, in school, in the neighborhood, and so on? Identify its good points and how it operates. Has anyone ever acted as the principal in this essay, calling you to consider the common good?

2. Are there issues currently troubling your community which might be resolved for everyone's benefit if the pillar of the common good were given greater weight? Explore.

3. How do the twin pillars of morality, the good of the individual and the good of the community, apply to the death penalty?

4. Many societal issues, both local and global, are mentioned in this chapter. List them and then rank them as to the urgency with which they should be addressed.

Which ones are most detrimental to the common good? Why? Name an issue that challenges the common good, an issue that this chapter does not mention.

5. The principle of the common good is dynamic, always in need of application as situations change. Look back into history to find an example of an issue relating to the common good which we no longer face in the same way today.

# I will challenge forces inimical to the common good

- by asking hard questions about immoral private behaviors which have significant negative public impact.

- by searching out what I can do to effect positive change in one current issue.

## Personal reflection

# How Are
# *the Children?*

A recent *Star Tribune* featured the Fourth Annual March for Peace
on the north side. An estimated 350 neighbors and friends demon-
strated their commitment to their community and to its residents.
I missed the march because of another commitment but was able
to attend the evening banquet, a truly memorable event.

Hosted at the Phyllis Wheatley Community Center, the First
Annual Elderhood Recognition and Awards banquet was born.
The banquet room was warmly decorated, the smiles on the
greeters' faces exuded hospitality, and the sound of an African
drumbeat filled the air. Along the walls hung photos of several
heroes and heroines of the African American community. A large
portrait of Ruby L. Hughes looked out on the gathered participants, enshrined with colorful cloth. Ruby Hughes died on the eve
of the first March for Peace, a victim of domestic violence.

A respected elder of the African American community, Sister
Hughes spent nearly thirty years advocating for disadvantaged chil-
dren and families. She had founded and directed La Creche Early
Childhood Centers, one of the first early childhood centers in
Minnesota. Revering her as a patient teacher, nurturing mentor,
loving mother, grandmother, sister, and friend, the West Broadway
Avenue March for Peace and Social Justice Foundation established
its outstanding Citizenship Award in her honor.

The participants at this event were mostly blacks. It was a wonderful celebration of what is best in human nature. From beginning
to end, the human spirit in its simplest nobility was highlighted—
from the opening invocation by a Christian pastor, followed by a

dinner served by men in the audience. Then came brief slices of inspiring music, rituals, and speeches.

The focus was on the wisdom of the elders. I was touched by the reflection titled, "The Backs Upon Which We Stand," a meditation by an elder from Ghana, garbed in colorful costume. He spoke eloquently about the need for the young to treasure their elders and to receive their wisdom. He reminded us that caring, sharing, and self-sacrifice are the three legs which hold up the stool of community. His words about freedom, especially freedom from fear, rang all too true. Coming from a village where people were free to fly and birds were kept in a cage, he found the opposite to be true in neighborhoods shackled by the threat of crime and violence.

Another speaker, one of the awardees, affirmed powerfully that "the struggle is all about the children." He reported that the Masai tribe in Africa has the custom of greeting one another, not with "How are you?" but "How are the children?" They know that if the children are all right, the adults will be all right also. Recognized for his endurance in the struggle for justice, beginning in the 1960s and continuing ever since, this elder gave witness to the beauty of a lifelong commitment to justice. The struggle is all about the children, handing on to them the best that we have.

The evening closed with everyone, hand to hand, in a circle with our backs against the walls. As I stood there, trying to grasp the significance of this simple gesture, I realized how appropriate was the poem by an African writer. "There is a dream in this land with its back against the wall. If the dream is to be saved for one, it's got to be saved for all." A memorable evening, celebrating God's gifts which come from Elderhood. The Spirit is alive. Praise God!

*Now the whole group of those who believed were of one heart and soul, and no one claimed private ownership of any possessions, but everything they owned was held in common.*

**Acts 4:32**

# From the Catholic Tradition

*If our nation is to be a land of opportunity for every child, then we must remove the serious educational and developmental disadvantages that are faced by students from poor families. These are not merely educational problems. They reflect the multiple effects of poverty, inadequate nutrition, poor health, and stressful, unsafe living conditions. Such factors combine to condemn many poor children to lives of poverty and ignorance.*

*Despite the complexity of these issues, we must resist the temptation to believe that nothing can be done to solve them. We are a strong and resourceful nation, and most poor families, given a decent chance, make determined and sometimes heroic efforts to lift themselves out of poverty.*

**Archbishop John R. Roach, *Reviving the Common Good*, Pastoral Letter on Social Justice.**

# For discussion

1. Wisdom is most often found in, although not limited to, the elders of a community. What does your community do to receive the wisdom of the elders? What more could it do to preserve that wisdom source?

2. Do you agree that if the children are all right, the adults will be all right also? What evidence is there that children in your community are all right? What evidence indicates that all is not well with the children?

3. How does the African poem given in this essay reflect the traditional wisdom of the common good?

4. Who in your community would you honor with an Elderhood Recognition Award? Why does this person deserve an award in your opinion? How does your "honoree" demonstrate caring, sharing and self-sacrifice?

5. What can free those imprisoned in neighborhoods shackled by threats of crime and violence?

# I will thank those who build up the common good

- by recognizing the contributions of the unsung heroic.
- by writing one thank you note a week, singling out various citizens who are dedicated to the good of all.

# Personal reflection

# Appendix

## A Prayer from the Heart of the Community

Creator God,
you have placed within us
a yearning only your love can satisfy.
It is you
who call us to homes of safety
and tables of friendship,
to neighborhoods of caring
and nations of civility.
Deepen within our hearts
our commitment to the common good
lest anyone be excluded,
sustain our compassion
until our tasks are done,
and unite us
under the banner of moral courage.
May we be drenched
in your rays of justice and compassion,
strengthened for the work before us.
For unless you build the city,
our constructs are in vain.
We humbly ask for your guidance.
Amen.

## A Prayer for the City

Creator God,
Source of vitality and freedom,
you call us beyond our limits.
So downward we tunnel,
upward we construct,
and sideward we reach out,
determined to connect.
Bless the constructs of our minds,
may they manifest your wisdom.
Nourish the feelings in our hearts,
may they express your compassion.
Bless the works of our hands,
may they reveal your justice.
For if we build without you,
we toil in vain.
In truth, we are the clay
and you are the potter.
Amen.

# *Prayer and Fasting*
## *for the City*

On October 14, 1996, more than 750 men and women began to fast and pray for the city of Minneapolis. They committed themselves to these spiritual works for the building up of the city's moral fabric, and the strengthening of the common good. Their commitment was for a period of 40 weeks, from October 14, 1996 to July 14, 1997.

Each week a particular segment of the city was the focus of the prayer and fasting.

If you, your friends, or your Church would like to initiate a similar effort, feel free to use the list on the next pages. Adopt it as is or adapt as you like.

Never underestimate the power of genuine prayer and the spiritual impact of fasting!

**Prayer:** Commit to a significant time for prayer, using whatever form or style appeals to your heart.

**Fasting:** Commit to a fast which is substantial but not harmful to your health. Three half meals with nothing in between is one suggestion. Listen to what hunger alone can teach.

# Scripture Reading

| Week | Focus | Scripture |
|------|-------|-----------|
| 1 | Teachers | Galatians 6:6–10 |
| 2 | Police | Jeremiah 33:10–13 |
| 3 | School principals | Ephesians 2:19–22 |
| 4 | Social workers | Romans 12:9–21 |
| 5 | Neighborhood leaders | 2 Corinthians 4:7–14 |
| 6 | Clergy of all faiths | 2 Timothy 1:6–14 |
| 7 | Business owners | Sirach 7:1–7 |
| 8 | Medical professionals | Sirach 38:1–8 |
| 9 | Attorneys | Sirach 15:1–10 |
| 10 | Philanthropists | 1 Timothy 6:17–19 |
| 11 | Coaches and counselors | Sirach 37:16–25 |
| 12 | Parents | Sirach 3:1–9 |
| 13 | Youth workers | 1 Timothy 4:11–16 |
| 14 | Grandparents/godparents | Sirach 6:24–28, 32–36 |
| 15 | Foster parents | Romans 8:22–27 |
| 16 | Single parents | 1 Corinthians 13:1–7 |
| 17 | Firefighters | Sirach 4:1–10 |
| 18 | Neighbors and citizens | Acts 2:42–46 |
| 19 | Relatives and friends | Sirach 6:5–17 |
| 20 | Tradesmen and women | Sirach 38:28–34 |
| 21 | Restaurant workers | Sirach 34:13–17 |
| 22 | Mentors | Philippians 4:4–9 |
| 23 | Volunteers | Colossians 1:24–29 |
| 24 | Office workers | Sirach 2:1–11 |
| 25 | Musicians | 1 Samuel 16:19–23 |
| 26 | Artists | Song of Songs 4:12–16 |
| 27 | Journalists | Sirach 18:14–20 |
| 28 | Judges | Acts 19:35–40 |
| 29 | County commissioners | Job 29:12–17 |

| 30 | Probation officers | James 1:22–27 |
| 31 | Welfare workers | Ephesians 4:1–6, 17–24 |
| 32 | Parks/playground workers | 1 Corinthians 9:24–27 |
| 33 | Computer technicians | Acts 20:28–35 |
| 34 | Scientists | Sirach 24:28–31 |
| 35 | Bishops | Titus 1:5–9 |
| 36 | Printers | 1 Peter 3:8–12 |
| 37 | Lab technicians | 1 John 4:7–12 |
| 38 | Professors | 1 Peter 4:7–11 |
| 39 | Pharmacists | Galatians 6:1–10 |
| 40 | City officials | Sirach 10:1–5 |